THE AUSTRALIAN Women's Weekly

100 meals in minutes

acp
books

contents

The oven temperatures in this book are for fan-forced ovens. If you have a conventional oven, increase the temperature by 10-20 degrees.
The imperial measurements used in these recipes are approximate only and should not affect your cooking results. A conversion chart appears on the inside cover flap.

starters

carpaccio with fresh herbs

500g (1 pound) piece beef eye-fillet, about
    6cm (2¼ inches) diameter
⅓ cup (80ml) extra virgin olive oil
¼ cup (60ml) lemon juice
¼ cup firmly packed fresh basil leaves
¼ cup firmly packed fresh flat-leaf parsley leaves
1 tablespoon fresh oregano leaves
1 tablespoon coarsely chopped fresh chives
¼ cup (25g) drained sun-dried tomatoes, sliced thinly
2 tablespoons flaked parmesan cheese

1 Remove any excess fat from beef. Wrap beef tightly in plastic wrap; freeze 1½ hours or until partly frozen.
2 Cut beef into paper-thin 1mm (¹⁄₁₆ inch) thick slices; freeze until required.
3 Just before serving, place beef on serving plate; drizzle with oil and juice, then top with combined herbs, tomato, and cheese.

prep & cook time 25 minutes (+ freezing) **serves** 8
nutritional count per serving 11.7g total fat
(2.3g saturated fat); 719kJ (172 cal);
1.3g carbohydrate; 15.1g protein; 0.6g fibre
notes Sashimi-quality tuna can be used in place of the beef; ask the fishmonger to slice it paper-thin for you. Omit the parmesan and add a sprinkling of baby capers.

bagna cauda

2⅔ cups (600ml) thickened (heavy) cream
60g (2 ounces) butter
45g (1½ ounces) anchovy fillets, drained,
    chopped finely
2 cloves garlic, crushed

1   Place cream in small saucepan; bring to the boil.
Reduce heat to low; simmer, uncovered, about
15 minutes or until cream thickens, stirring frequently.
2   Meanwhile, melt butter over low heat in medium
saucepan, taking care not to brown butter. Add anchovy
and garlic; stir until mixture is combined and becomes
paste-like.
3   Stir hot cream into anchovy mixture until well
combined; serve warm.

prep & cook time 25 minutes **makes** 2¾ cups
nutritional count per tablespoon 8.4g total fat
(5.5g saturated fat); 334kJ (80 cal);
0.6g carbohydrate; 0.8g protein; 0g fibre
note Bagna cauda is a warm dip; you can serve it
in a fondue pot with a small tea light or gentle flame
underneath. Serve the dip with your favourite selection
of crisp vegetables.

baked mushrooms

9 medium flat mushrooms (900g)
60g (2 ounces) butter, melted
3 rindless bacon slices (195g), chopped finely
4 green onions (scallions), chopped finely
2 cloves garlic, crushed
2 tablespoons stale breadcrumbs
1 tablespoon pouring cream
2 teaspoons fresh oregano, chopped coarsely
2 tablespoons grated parmesan cheese

1   Gently remove stalks from eight mushrooms. Chop stalks and the remaining mushroom finely.
2   Brush mushroom caps all over with butter. Place on lightly oiled oven trays.
3   Preheat oven to 180°C/350°F.
4   Cook bacon and onion in heated oiled small frying pan until bacon is crisp. Add chopped mushroom, garlic and breadcrumbs. Cook, stirring, until well combined. Remove from heat; stir in cream, oregano and cheese. Divide bacon mixture between mushroom caps.
5   Bake, in oven, about 10 minutes or until hot.

prep & cook time 25 minutes **serves** 4
nutritional count per serving 22.9g total fat
(12.7g saturated fat); 1321kJ (316 cal);
5.8g carbohydrate; 19.5g protein; 6.1g fibre
note Cap mushrooms can be substituted for the flat mushrooms. Cook 5 minutes; cool slightly before serving.

baked mussels

24 small black mussels (500g)
¾ cup (180ml) water
¼ cup (60ml) olive oil
1 clove garlic, crushed
2 tablespoons finely chopped fresh flat-leaf parsley
½ cup (35g) stale breadcrumbs
1 medium tomato (130g), deseeded, chopped finely

1 Scrub mussels, remove beards. Heat the water in large saucepan, add mussels; cook, covered, over high heat about 3 minutes or until shells open (discard any that do not). Drain; discard liquid.
2 Loosen mussels; remove from shell. Discard one half of each shell; reserve remaining half. Combine mussel meat, oil, garlic, parsley and breadcrumbs in small bowl; mix well. Cover; refrigerate 30 minutes.
3 Preheat oven to 200°C/400°F.
4 Place one mussel in each shell; place on oven tray. Combine tomato with breadcrumb mixture; spoon over mussels. Bake about 5 minutes or until breadcrumbs are browned lightly.

prep & cook time 30 minutes (+ refrigeration) **serves** 4
nutritional count per serving 14.5g total fat
(2.1g saturated fat); 744kJ (178 cal);
7.5g carbohydrate; 4.4g protein; 0.8g fibre

chilli scallops

1 tablespoon peanut oil
32 small scallops with the roe attached (1.3kg)
4 cloves garlic, sliced thinly
5cm (2 inch) piece fresh ginger (25g), sliced thinly
2 fresh small red thai (serrano) chillies, chopped finely
3 green onions (scallions), sliced thinly
⅓ cup (80ml) sweet chilli sauce
1 teaspoon fish sauce
2 teaspoons light brown sugar
½ cup (125ml) chicken stock
¼ cup loosely packed, finely chopped
   fresh coriander (cilantro)

1   Heat half the oil in wok; stir-fry scallops, in batches, until just changed in colour. Remove from wok.
2   Heat remaining oil in wok; stir-fry garlic, ginger, chilli and onion until onion is soft.
3   Stir in combined sauces, sugar and stock; bring to the boil. Return scallops to wok; stir until heated through. Serve scallops sprinkled with coriander.

prep & cook time 30 minutes serves 4
nutritional count per serving 7.6g total fat
(1.7g saturated fat); 1091kJ (261 cal);
8.3g carbohydrate; 38.7g protein; 1.6g fibre
notes We used scallops with the roe attached but the roe can be left out if you prefer. If you buy scallops in their shell, don't discard the shell; they are great (washed and dried) to use as serving dishes.

roast capsicum & prosciutto bruschetta

½ loaf ciabatta bread (275g)
3 cloves garlic, halved
¼ cup (60ml) olive oil
2 medium red capsicums (bell pepper) (400g)
5 slices prosciutto (75g), chopped coarsely
1 tablespoon balsamic vinegar
2 tablespoons fresh oregano leaves

1   Preheat grill (broiler). Cut bread into 1.5cm (½ inch) thick slices; halve any large slices crossways. Toast under hot grill until browned lightly; while still hot, rub one side of toast with garlic. Place toast on tray; drizzle oil evenly over toast.
2   Quarter capsicums; discard seeds and membranes. Roast under grill, skin-side up, until skin blisters and blackens. Cover capsicum pieces with plastic or paper 5 minutes; peel away skin then cut into thin strips.
3   Heat oiled medium frying pan; cook prosciutto until crisp. Add capsicum and vinegar to pan; stir to combine. Cool to room temperature.
4   Just before serving, divide capsicum mixture among bruschetta; top with oregano.

prep & cook time 30 minutes **serves 8**
nutritional count per serving 8.4g total fat
(1.3g saturated fat); 711kJ (170 cal);
17.3g carbohydrate; 5.4g protein; 2.3g fibre

creamy mushroom bruschetta

½ loaf ciabatta bread (275g)
4 cloves garlic, halved
½ cup (125ml) olive oil
250g flat mushrooms, chopped finely
1 tablespoon lemon juice
½ cup (125ml) pouring cream
125g button mushrooms, sliced thinly
2 tablespoons finely grated parmesan cheese
¼ cup coarsely chopped fresh chives

1   Preheat grill (broiler). Cut bread into 1.5cm (½ inch) thick slices; halve any large slices crossways. Toast under hot grill until browned lightly; while still hot, rub one side of each toast using three cloves of the garlic. Place toast on tray; drizzle half the oil evenly over toast.
2   Crush remaining garlic. Heat remaining oil in medium frying pan; cook flat mushrooms and garlic until very soft. Add juice; stir over high heat until absorbed. Stir in cream. Stir in button mushrooms over high heat until almost all liquid is absorbed. Remove from heat; stir in cheese.
3   Just before serving, top bruschetta with mushroom mixture; sprinkle with chives.

prep & cook time 35 minutes **serves 8**
nutritional count per serving 22.6g total fat
(7g saturated fat); 1241kJ (297 cal);
16.8g carbohydrate; 5.7g protein; 3g fibre

olive, anchovy & caper bruschetta

½ loaf ciabatta bread (275g)
3 cloves garlic, halved
⅓ cup (80ml) olive oil
3 drained anchovy fillets, chopped finely
½ cup (60g) seeded black olives, chopped finely
1 tablespoon rinsed, drained baby capers
1 tablespoon lemon juice
⅓ cup (25g) parmesan cheese flakes
2 tablespoons fresh marjoram leaves

1   Preheat grill (broiler). Cut bread into 1.5cm (½ inch) thick slices; halve any large slices crossways. Toast under hot grill until browned lightly; while still hot, rub one side of toast with garlic. Place toast on tray; drizzle ¼ cup of the oil evenly over toast.
2   Combine anchovy, olives, capers, juice and remaining oil in small bowl.
3   Just before serving, divide olive mixture among bruschetta; top with cheese then marjoram.

prep & cook time 20 minutes serves 8
nutritional count per serving 12g total fat
(2.2g saturated fat); 882kJ (221 cal);
20.1g carbohydrate; 4.9g protein; 2.2g fibre

tomato & rocket bruschetta

½ loaf ciabatta bread (275g)
3 cloves garlic, halved
¼ cup (60ml) olive oil
3 medium egg (plum) tomatoes (225g), chopped finely
½ small red onion (50g), chopped finely
25g baby rocket leaves (arugula)

1   Preheat grill (broiler). Cut bread into 1.5cm (½ inch) thick slices; halve any large slices crossways. Toast under hot grill until browned lightly; while still hot, rub one side of toast with garlic. Place toast on tray; drizzle oil evenly over toast.
2   Combine tomato and onion in small bowl.
3   Just before serving, top bruschetta with tomato mixture then rocket.

prep & cook time 20 minutes serves 8
nutritional count per serving 8.3g total fat
(1.2g saturated fat); 715kJ (171 cal);
19.1g carbohydrate; 3.7g protein; 2.5g fibre

tomatoes & goat's cheese in walnut dressing

8 medium vine-ripened tomatoes (1.5kg), sliced thickly
150g (5 ounces) goat's cheese, sliced thickly
¼ cup (25g) walnuts, roasted, chopped coarsely
¼ cup (60ml) olive oil
1 clove garlic, crushed
1½ tablespoons raspberry vinegar
2 teaspoons dijon mustard
2 teaspoons coarsely chopped fresh thyme
2 teaspoons white sugar

1 Place a slice of tomato on each serving plate; top with a slice of cheese.
2 Repeat, sprinkling nuts and combined remaining ingredients between layers.

prep & cook time 15 minutes **serves** 6
nutritional count per serving 16.2g total fat (4.1g saturated fat); 857kJ (205 cal); 6.6g carbohydrate; 6.5g protein; 3.4g fibre
notes Hazelnuts can be substituted for walnuts and, if you have hazelnut or walnut oil at hand, use one of these rather than the olive oil.
Sample a few different goat's cheeses before you decide on one; they vary greatly in texture and taste.

prosciutto-wrapped haloumi

120g (4 ounce) piece haloumi cheese
8 slices prosciutto (120g)
2 tablespoons coarsely chopped fresh flat-leaf parsley
1 teaspoon lemon juice

1   Cut cheese into eight fingers. Wrap each finger in
a slice of prosciutto, securing ends with toothpicks.
2   Cook on heated oiled grill plate (or grill or barbecue)
about 8 minutes or until browned all over. Serve
sprinkled with parsley and juice.

prep & cook time 15 minutes serves 4
nutritional count per serving 6.9g total fat
(3.9g saturated fat); 468kJ (112 cal);
0.7g carbohydrate; 11.9g protein; 0.1g fibre

soups

green pea soup with mint pistou

1 tablespoon olive oil
1 small leek (200g), sliced thinly
1 clove garlic, crushed
2 large potatoes (600g), chopped coarsely
3 cups (360g) frozen peas
3 cups (750ml) water
2 cups (500ml) vegetable stock
mint pistou
2 cups loosely packed fresh mint leaves
¼ cup (20g) finely grated parmesan cheese
1 tablespoon lemon juice
1 clove garlic, quartered
¼ cup (60ml) olive oil

1 Heat oil in large saucepan; cook leek and garlic, stirring, until leek softens. Add potato, peas, the water and stock; bring to the boil. Reduce heat; simmer, covered, about 10 minutes or until potato is tender. Cool 10 minutes.
2 Meanwhile, make mint pistou.
3 Blend or process soup, in batches, until smooth. Return soup to same cleaned pan; stir over medium heat until hot.
4 Serve bowls of soup topped with pistou.
mint pistou Blend or process ingredients until smooth.

prep & cook time 30 minutes serves 4
nutritional count per serving 21.3g total fat (3.9g saturated fat); 1542kJ (369 cal); 25.8g carbohydrate; 13.2g protein; 11.7g fibre

chicken, corn & noodle chowder

1 medium brown onion (150g), chopped coarsely
2 cloves garlic, crushed
420g (13 ounces) canned corn kernels, rinsed, drained
750g (24 ounces) canned small potatoes, rinsed,
    drained, quartered
1 litre (4 cups) chicken stock
375g (12 ounces) chicken tenderloins,
    chopped coarsely
150g (5 ounces) fresh egg noodles
2 tablespoons low-fat sour cream

1 Heat oiled large saucepan; cook onion and garlic,
stirring, until onion softens. Add corn, potato and stock,
bring to the boil then simmer, covered, 10 minutes.
2 Stand potato mixture 10 minutes, then blend or
process, in batches, until smooth. Return potato mixture
to same pan, add chicken and noodles; simmer,
uncovered, about 10 minutes or until chicken is tender.
3 Serve with sour cream; top with finely sliced fresh
herbs, if desired.

prep & cook time 30 minutes serves 4
nutritional count per serving 6.9g total fat
(3.2g saturated fat); 1601kJ (383 cal);
44.8g carbohydrate; 31.9g protein; 6.1g fibre

minted lamb & vermicelli soup

100g (3½ ounces) bean thread vermicelli
1 tablespoon peanut oil
600g (1¼ pounds) lamb fillets, sliced thinly
2 tablespoons finely chopped fresh lemon grass
2 teaspoons bottled chopped chilli
8cm (3 inch) piece fresh ginger (40g), grated
4 cloves garlic, crushed
⅓ cup (80ml) fish sauce
1.5 litres (6 cups) chicken stock
1 tablespoon white sugar
500g (1 pound) asparagus, trimmed, chopped coarsely
¼ cup finely chopped fresh coriander (cilantro)
⅓ cup finely chopped fresh mint
8 green onions (scallions), chopped finely
4 medium tomatoes (760g), deseeded, sliced thinly

1 Place vermicelli in large heatproof bowl, cover with boiling water; stand until just tender, drain.
2 Meanwhile, heat half the oil in large saucepan; cook lamb, in batches, until browned. Remove from pan.
3 Heat remaining oil in same pan; cook lemon grass, chilli, ginger and garlic, stirring, until fragrant. Add sauce, stock and sugar; cook, stirring, until mixture boils.
4 Add asparagus; simmer, uncovered, until asparagus is just tender. Add herbs, onion, tomato, vermicelli and lamb to pan; stir until soup is hot.

prep & cook time 30 minutes serves 6
nutritional count per serving 10g total fat
(3.2g saturated fat); 1041kJ (249 cal);
11.1g carbohydrate; 27.6g protein; 2.4g fibre

17

pumpkin soup

40g (1¼ ounces) butter
1 large brown onion (200g), chopped coarsely
3 rindless bacon slices (195g), chopped coarsely
1.5kg (3 pounds) pumpkin, chopped coarsely
2 large potatoes (600g), chopped coarsely
1.5 litres (6 cups) chicken stock

1   Melt butter in large saucepan; cook onion and bacon, stirring, until onion softens. Stir in pumpkin and potato.
2   Stir in stock; bring to the boil. Reduce heat; simmer, uncovered, about 20 minutes or until pumpkin is soft.
3   Stand soup 10 minutes, then blend or process soup, in batches, until smooth. Return to same cleaned pan; stir until heated through.

prep & cook time 35 minutes serves 6
nutritional count per serving 10.3g total fat
(5.8g saturated fat); 1166kJ (279 cal);
28.1g carbohydrate; 16.3g protein; 4.3g fibre

tomato & borlotti soup

2 medium brown onions (300g), chopped coarsely
2 cloves garlic, crushed
1kg (2 pounds) large egg (plum) tomatoes,
    chopped coarsely
2 cups (500ml) chicken stock
1 tablespoon worcestershire sauce
2 tablespoons finely chopped fresh flat-leaf parsley
800g (30 ounces) canned borlotti beans,
    rinsed, drained

1   Heat oiled large saucepan; cook onion and garlic, stirring, until onion softens.
2   Add tomato to pan; cook, stirring, about 3 minutes or until tomato softens. Add stock and sauce, bring to the boil. Reduce heat; simmer, covered, 15 minutes.
3   Stand tomato mixture 10 minutes, then blend or process, in batches, until almost smooth. Return tomato mixture to pan, stir in parsley and beans; simmer, uncovered, about 5 minutes or until hot.

prep & cook time 30 minutes serves 4
nutritional count per serving 1.4g total fat
(0.4g saturated fat); 861kJ (206 cal);
29.2g carbohydrate; 13.4g protein; 12.3g fibre

chunky vegetable & pasta soup

1 tablespoon olive oil
2 medium brown onions (300g), chopped finely
2 cloves garlic, crushed
4 stalks celery (600g), trimmed, chopped finely
2 medium carrots (240g), chopped finely
1⅔ cups (410g) canned tomato puree
⅓ cup (90g) tomato paste
420g (15 ounces) canned kidney beans, rinsed, drained
3 litres (12 cups) chicken stock
500g (1 pound) penne pasta
¼ cup finely chopped fresh flat-leaf parsley

1 Heat oil in large saucepan; cook onion, garlic, celery and carrot, stirring, until onion softens.
2 Add tomato puree, paste, beans and stock; bring to the boil.
3 Add pasta; boil, uncovered, until pasta is tender. Serve soup sprinkled with parsley.

prep & cook time 35 minutes serves 6
nutritional count per serving 6.9g total fat (1.8g saturated fat); 2073kJ (496 cal); 80.1g carbohydrate; 22.3g protein; 10.3g fibre
note The pasta will absorb the liquid as it stands, so if preparing ahead, more stock may need to be added on reheating.

tomato, capsicum & cannellini soup

1 tablespoon olive oil
2 medium brown onions (300g), chopped coarsely
1 large red capsicum (350g), chopped coarsely
1 fresh long red chilli, chopped finely
810g (28 ounces) canned crushed tomatoes
1 litre (4 cups) chicken stock
600g (20 ounces) canned cannellini beans, rinsed, drained

1 Heat oil in large saucepan; cook onion, capsicum and chilli, stirring, until vegetables are very soft. Add undrained tomatoes and stock; bring to the boil. Reduce heat; simmer, covered, about 15 minutes or until soup is thickened slightly.
2 Stand soup 10 minutes, then blend or process soup, in batches, until smooth; return to same cleaned pan. Add beans; stir until hot. Accompany with garlic bread, if you like.

prep & cook time 30 minutes serves 6
nutritional count per serving 4.5g total fat (0.9g saturated fat); 665kJ (159 cal); 18.4g carbohydrate; 8.6g protein; 7.2g fibre
note Cannellini beans are also known as butter beans. You can also use kidney beans, chickpeas or small pasta.

asian mushroom broth

cooking-oil spray
4 green onions (scallions), chopped finely
1 stalk celery (150g), trimmed, chopped finely
1.5 litres (6 cups) chicken stock
1½ cups (375ml) water
¼ cup (60ml) light soy sauce
100g (3¾ ounces) shiitake mushrooms, sliced thinly
100g (3¾ ounces) enoki mushrooms, trimmed
150g (5 ounces) oyster mushrooms, sliced thinly
150g (5 ounces) swiss brown mushrooms, sliced thinly
½ teaspoon five-spice powder
2 tablespoons finely chopped fresh garlic chives

1   Spray heated large saucepan with oil; cook onion
and celery, stirring, until vegetables soften.
2   Add stock, the water and sauce; bring to the boil. Add
mushrooms and five-spice; return to the boil. Reduce
heat; simmer 2 minutes or until mushrooms soften.
3   Just before serving, sprinkle with chives.

prep & cook time 20 minutes serves 4
nutritional count per serving 2.4g total fat
(0.8g saturated fat); 376kJ (90 cal);
5.6g carbohydrate; 8.7g protein; 3.6g fibre
note Other varieties of mushrooms, such as button or
shimeji, can also be used in this recipe.

lentil & spinach soup

2 tablespoons peanut oil
2 large brown onions (400g), chopped finely
2 cloves garlic, crushed
2 teaspoons ground cumin
1 teaspoon ground turmeric
1 teaspoon ground coriander
3 cups (600g) red lentils
1.25 litres (5 cups) chicken stock
1 litre (4 cups) water
500g (1 pound) spinach, trimmed, chopped finely

1   Heat oil in large saucepan; cook onion and garlic, stirring, until onion is soft. Add spices; cook, stirring, until fragrant. Stir in lentils.
2   Add stock and the water; bring to the boil. Reduce heat; simmer, uncovered, about 20 minutes or until lentils are tender.
3   Stand soup 10 minutes, then blend or process soup, in batches, until smooth. Return soup to same cleaned pan, add spinach; stir over heat until hot.

prep & cook time 35 minutes serves 8
nutritional count per serving 6.9g total fat
(1.4g saturated fat); 1225kJ (293 cal);
32.5g carbohydrate; 21.4g protein; 11.9g fibre

cream of zucchini soup

30g (1 ounce) butter
1 large brown onion (200g), chopped finely
2 cloves garlic, crushed
2 tablespoons plain (all-purpose) flour
8 large zucchini (1.2kg), chopped coarsely
1½ cups (375ml) chicken stock
1 cup (250ml) water
½ cup (125ml) pouring cream

1 Melt butter in large saucepan; cook onion and garlic, stirring, until onion softens. Add flour and zucchini; cook, stirring, 2 minutes.
2 Stir in stock and the water, bring to the boil. Reduce heat; simmer, uncovered, about 15 minutes or until zucchini is tender.
3 Stand soup 10 minutes, then blend or process soup, in batches, until smooth.
4 Just before serving, return soup to same cleaned pan. Add cream; stir over medium heat until hot. Serve topped with chervil, if you like.

prep & cook time 35 minutes **serves** 4
nutritional count per serving 21.1g total fat (13.2g saturated fat); 1162kJ (278 cal); 13.3g carbohydrate; 6.7g protein; 5.9g fibre

tomato, corn & chilli chicken soup

2 tablespoons olive oil
2 chicken breast fillets (400g)
1 medium red onion (170g), chopped finely
1 tablespoon plain (all-purpose) flour
1.5 litres (6 cups) chicken stock
2 cups (500ml) tomato juice
420g (13 ounces) canned corn kernels, drained
2 fresh small red thai (serrano) chillies, chopped finely
¼ cup loosely packed fresh coriander (cilantro) leaves

1 Heat half the oil in large saucepan; cook chicken until cooked through. When cool enough to handle, shred chicken into small pieces.

2 Heat remaining oil in same pan; cook onion, stirring, until soft. Add flour; cook, stirring, until mixture bubbles and thickens. Gradually stir in stock and juice; cook, stirring, until mixture boils and thickens slightly.

3 Add chicken, corn and chilli; stir over heat until soup is hot. Just before serving, sprinkle with coriander.

prep & cook time 30 minutes **serves** 6
nutritional count per serving 8.6g total fat
(1.7g saturated fat); 957kJ (229 cal);
18.3g carbohydrate; 18.3g protein; 2.6g fibre
note A ready-cooked chicken can be substituted for the chicken breasts; discard skin, excess fat and all bones before shredding the meat.

rice & noodles

chilli prawn & noodle salad

250g (8 ounces) cooked medium king prawns
   (shrimp)
¼ cup (60ml) lime juice
2 tablespoons sweet chilli sauce
1 fresh long red chilli, sliced thinly
1 long green chilli, sliced thinly
2 teaspoons white sugar
200g (6½ ounces) bean thread noodles
2 tablespoons finely shredded fresh mint leaves

1 Shell and devein prawns leaving tails intact. Combine prawns with juice, sauce, chillies and sugar in large bowl.
2 Place noodles in large heatproof bowl, cover with boiling water; stand until tender, drain.
3 Combine noodles and mint with prawn mixture.

prep & cook time 30 minutes **serves** 4
nutritional count per serving 0.9g total fat
(0.2g saturated fat); 439kJ (105 cal);
14.2g carbohydrate; 8.8g protein; 1.2g fibre

fried rice with prawns

6 dried shiitake mushrooms
500g (1 pound) uncooked medium king prawns
  (shrimp)
1 tablespoon peanut oil
1 medium brown onion (150g), sliced thinly
1 teaspoon sesame oil
1 clove garlic, crushed
4cm (1½ inch) piece fresh ginger (20g), grated
1 medium red capsicum (bell pepper) (200g),
  chopped coarsely
1 medium carrot (120g), sliced thinly
2 stalks celery (300g), trimmed, sliced thinly
100g snow peas
500g (1 pound) packet pre-cooked rice
1 cup (80g) bean sprouts
6 green onions (scallions), sliced thinly
¼ cup (60ml) oyster sauce
¼ cup (60ml) hoisin sauce
1 tablespoon fish sauce

1 Cover mushrooms with boiling water in heatproof bowl;
stand 10 minutes, drain. Discard stems; slice caps finely.
2 Shell and devein prawns, leaving tails intact.
3 Heat half the peanut oil in wok; stir-fry brown onion
until soft. Add sesame oil, garlic, ginger and prawns,
stir-fry until prawns change colour; remove from wok.
4 Heat remaining peanut oil in wok, add capsicum, carrot,
celery and peas; stir-fry until vegetables are just tender.
5 Return prawn mixture to wok with mushroom, rice,
sprouts, green onion and sauces; stir-fry until hot.

prep & cook time 30 minutes serves 4
nutritional count per serving 7.8g total fat
(1.2g saturated fat); 1597kJ (382 cal);
53.7g carbohydrate; 20.3g protein; 6.5g fibre
tip Instead of packaged pre-cooked rice, cook 2½ cups
long-grain rice; spread on tray, cover with absorbent
paper and refrigerate overnight.

spicy chicken fried rice

2 teaspoons peanut oil

2 eggs, beaten lightly

500g (1 pound) chicken thigh fillets, sliced thinly

2 medium brown onions (300g), chopped finely

1 tablespoon ground cumin

2 teaspoons ground coriander

¼ teaspoon cardamom seeds

1 teaspoon ground cinnamon

2 fresh small red thai (serrano) chillies, chopped finely

2 cloves garlic, crushed

1 large red capsicum (bell pepper) (350g), sliced thinly

115g fresh baby corn, halved lengthways

500g (1 pound) packet pre-cooked rice

4 green onions (scallions), sliced finely

2 tablespoons kecap manis

2 tablespoons coarsely chopped fresh coriander
   (cilantro) leaves

1 Heat ½ teaspoon of the oil in wok, add half the egg, swirl so egg forms a thin omelette; cook until set.

2 Transfer omelette to board, roll, cut into thin strips. Repeat with remaining egg and another ½ teaspoon oil.

3 Heat remaining oil in wok; stir-fry chicken and brown onion, in batches, until chicken is tender. Remove mixture from wok.

4 Add spices, chilli and garlic to wok; stir-fry until fragrant. Add capsicum and corn; stir-fry until just tender. Return chicken mixture to wok with omelette strips, rice, green onion, kecap manis and coriander; stir-fry until hot.

prep & cook time 30 minutes serves 4
nutritional count per serving 12.5g total fat
(3.2g saturated fat); 1881kJ (450 cal);
47.8g carbohydrate; 33.9g protein; 4.2g fibre
tip Instead of packaged pre-cooked rice, cook 2½ cups long-grain rice; spread on tray, cover with absorbent paper and refrigerate overnight.

pork, pine nut & cointreau risotto

500g (1 pound) pork fillets
1 tablespoon teriyaki marinade
1 teaspoon finely grated orange rind
3 cloves garlic, crushed
1 large brown onion (200g), chopped finely
2 cups (400g) arborio rice
1.25 litres (5 cups) chicken stock
½ cup (125ml) dry white wine
2 tablespoons cointreau
150g baby spinach leaves
2 tablespoons pine nuts, roasted
2 tablespoons coarsely chopped fresh lemon thyme

1 Preheat oven to 200°C/400°F.
2 Place pork on rack in baking dish; brush with combined marinade and rind. Bake, uncovered, 20 minutes. Cover pork, stand 5 minutes then slice thickly.
3 Meanwhile, cook garlic and onion in heated, oiled large saucepan, stirring, until onion softens. Add rice, stock, wine and liqueur; bring to the boil. Simmer, covered, 15 minutes, stirring halfway through cooking.
4 Remove risotto from heat; stand, covered, 10 minutes. Gently stir in spinach, pine nuts, thyme and pork.

prep & cook time 30 minutes serves 4
nutritional count per serving 10.5g total fat
(2.1g saturated fat); 2805kJ (671 cal);
90.4g carbohydrate; 40.3g protein; 3.3g fibre

mushroom, spinach & lemon risotto

2 medium brown onions (300g), chopped finely
3 cloves garlic, crushed
1 tablespoon finely grated lemon rind
300g (10 ounces) button mushrooms, halved
2 cups (400g) arborio rice
1.5 litres (6 cups) chicken stock
1 cup (250ml) dry white wine
300g baby spinach leaves
2 tablespoons coarsely chopped fresh lemon thyme

1 Heat oiled large saucepan; cook onion, garlic, rind and mushrooms, stirring, until mushrooms are browned lightly.
2 Add rice, stock and wine, bring to the boil; simmer, covered, 15 minutes, stirring halfway through cooking.
3 Remove from heat; stand, covered, 10 minutes. Gently stir in spinach and thyme.

prep & cook time 30 minutes serves 4
nutritional count per serving 2.6g total fat (0.9g saturated fat); 2082kJ (498 cal); 87.9g carbohydrate; 16.6g protein; 6.2g fibre

sesame chicken noodle salad

3 chicken breast fillets (600g), sliced
1 clove garlic, crushed
2 tablespoons sweet chilli sauce
½ teaspoon sesame oil
¼ cup (60ml) rice vinegar
2 tablespoons japanese soy sauce
1 tablespoon lemon juice
1 green onion (scallion), sliced finely
2 teaspoons white sugar
600g (1¼ pounds) fresh egg noodles
1 medium yellow capsicum (bell pepper) (200g)
1 large carrot (180g)
200g (6½ ounces) watercress, trimmed
1 tablespoon peanut oil
250g (8 ounces) asparagus, trimmed, halved
2 teaspoons sesame seeds, toasted

1   Combine chicken, garlic and sweet chilli sauce in large bowl.
2   For dressing, combine sesame oil, vinegar, soy sauce, juice, onion and sugar in screw-top jar; shake well.
3   Cook noodles in large saucepan of boiling water, uncovered, until just tender; drain.
4   Discard seeds and membranes from capsicum; cut capsicum and carrot into long thin strips. Combine noodles, capsicum, carrot and watercress in large bowl; mix well.
5   Heat peanut oil in wok; stir-fry chicken mixture, in batches, until browned and cooked through. Remove from wok. Add asparagus to wok; stir-fry until tender.
6   Combine chicken and asparagus with noodle mixture; drizzle with dressing, sprinkle with sesame seeds.

prep & cook time 30 minutes **serves** 6
nutritional count per serving 7g total fat (1.4g saturated fat); 1868kJ (447 cal); 57.8g carbohydrate; 34.4g protein; 4.6g fibre

sweet soy chicken & noodles

250g (8 ounces) soba noodles
1 tablespoon peanut oil
2 chicken breast fillets (600g), sliced thinly
200g (6½ ounces) sugar snap peas
2 tablespoons kecap manis
4 green onions (scallions), sliced thinly
6 red radishes (200g), sliced thinly
2 tablespoons finely chopped fresh
   coriander (cilantro)

1   Cook noodles in large saucepan of boiling water, uncovered, until just tender; drain. Rinse noodles under hot water; cover to keep warm.
2   Meanwhile, heat half the oil in wok; stir-fry chicken, in batches, until tender. Remove from wok. Heat remaining oil in wok, add peas; stir-fry until just tender. Return chicken to wok with sauce, onion and radish; cook, stirring, until hot.
3   Combine noodles and coriander in large bowl; serve topped with chicken mixture.

prep & cook time 30 minutes serves 4
nutritional count per serving 7.8g total fat
(1.7g saturated fat); 1835kJ (439 cal);
46.2g carbohydrate; 42.9 protein; 3.8g fibre
note Kecap manis, also known as ketjap manis, is a dark, thick, sweet soy sauce. Depending on the brand, the soy's sweetness is derived from the addition of either molasses or palm sugar when brewed.

lemon grass chicken with vermicelli salad

250g (8 ounces) bean thread vermicelli
1 tablespoon peanut oil
3 chicken thigh fillets (600g), sliced thinly
2 x 10cm (4 inch) sticks fresh lemon grass (40g), sliced thinly
1 clove garlic, crushed
1 tablespoon fish sauce
2 cups (120g) shredded iceberg lettuce
1 medium carrot (120g), cut into matchsticks
½ lebanese cucumber (130g), deseeded, sliced thinly
¼ cup (35g) coarsely chopped roasted unsalted peanuts
1 red radish (35g), trimmed, cut into thin strips
chilli dressing
¼ cup (75g) white sugar
½ cup (125ml) water
2 tablespoons white vinegar
1 fresh small red thai (seranno) chilli, chopped finely

1 Place vermicelli in medium heatproof bowl, cover with boiling water; stand until just tender, drain.
2 Meanwhile, make chilli dressing.
3 Heat oil in wok; stir-fry chicken, in batches, until browned. Return chicken to wok with lemon grass and garlic; cook, stirring, until lemon grass softens. Add sauce; stir-fry until hot.
4 Serve vermicelli with lettuce, carrot, cucumber and chicken mixture; sprinkle with nuts, radish and half the dressing. Serve with remaining dressing.
chilli dressing Combine sugar and the water in small saucepan; stir over low heat until sugar dissolves. Bring to the boil. Reduce heat; simmer, uncovered, about 5 minutes or until mixture thickens slightly. Remove from heat; stir in vinegar and chilli.

prep & cook time 30 minutes serves 4
nutritional count per serving 19.8g total fat (4.6g saturated fat); 1856kJ (444 cal); 33.7g carbohydrate; 32.2g protein; 2.7g fibre
note You will need about half a medium head of iceberg lettuce to get the amount required for this recipe.

thai chicken stir-fry

250g (8 ounces) dried rice stick noodles
3 chicken thigh fillets (600g), sliced thinly
⅓ cup (80ml) sweet chilli sauce
1 tablespoon peanut oil
300g (10 ounces) green beans, halved widthways
2 cloves garlic, crushed
2cm (¾ inch) piece fresh ginger (10g), grated
2 fresh small red thai (serrano) chillies, sliced thinly
2 tablespoons fish sauce
¼ cup (60ml) lime juice
6 green onions (scallions), chopped coarsely
2 cups (160g) bean sprouts
¼ cup firmly packed fresh coriander (cilantro) leaves
¼ cup firmly packed fresh mint leaves

1 Place noodles in large heatproof bowl, cover with boiling water; stand until just tender, drain.
2 Meanwhile, combine chicken and half the sweet chilli sauce in large bowl. Heat oil in wok; stir-fry chicken mixture, in batches. Remove from wok.
3 Add beans, garlic, ginger and half the chilli to wok; stir-fry until beans are tender.
4 Return chicken to wok with noodles and remaining ingredients; stir-fry until hot.

prep & cook time 30 minutes **serves** 4
nutritional count per serving 16.4g total fat
(4.2g saturated fat); 1555kJ (372 cal);
19.6g carbohydrate; 33.3g protein; 5.3g fibre

stir-fried prawns & noodles

500g (1 pound) uncooked medium king prawns
(shrimp)
200g (6½ ounces) dried rice stick noodles
1 clove garlic, crushed
2 tablespoons japanese soy sauce
2 tablespoons fish sauce
1 teaspoon sambal oelek
1 cup (80g) bean sprouts
¼ cup fresh coriander (cilantro) leaves

1   Shell and devein prawns leaving tails intact.
2   Place noodles in large heatproof bowl, cover with
boiling water; stand until just tender, drain.
3   Meanwhile, heat oiled wok; stir-fry prawns and garlic
until prawns are just changed in colour. Add noodles,
sauces and sambal; gently stir-fry until hot. Stir in bean
sprouts and coriander.

prep & cook time 30 minutes serves 4
nutritional count per serving 1.1g total fat
(0.1g saturated fat); 506kJ (121 cal);
11g carbohydrate; 15.7g protein; 1.2g fibre

teriyaki beef stir-fry

2 tablespoons peanut oil
2 teaspoons sesame oil
2 cloves garlic, sliced thinly
600g (1¼ pound) piece beef rump steak, sliced thinly
1 medium brown onion (150g), sliced thickly
230g (7 ounces) canned bamboo shoots, rinsed, drained
½ cup (40g) bean sprouts
¼ cup (60ml) teriyaki sauce
⅓ cup (80ml) beef stock
450g (14 ounces) hokkien noodles
4 green onions (scallions), sliced thickly

1 Heat oils in wok; stir-fry garlic and beef, in batches, until beef is browned. Remove from wok.
2 Stir-fry brown onion and bamboo shoots 2 minutes.
3 Return beef mixture to wok with bean sprouts. Stir in sauce and stock; stir-fry until mixture boils.
4 Meanwhile, place noodles in medium heatproof bowl, cover with boiling water; separate with fork, drain. Serve stir-fry with the noodles; sprinkle with green onions.

prep & cook time 35 minutes serves 4
nutritional count per serving 21.2g total fat
(5.4g saturated fat); 2646kJ (633 cal);
63.1g carbohydrate; 44.8g protein; 3.9g fibre

beef in black bean sauce with rice noodles & greens

250g (8 ounces) dried rice stick noodles
1 tablespoon peanut oil
600g (1¼ pounds) minced (ground) beef
1 medium brown onion (150g), sliced thinly
2 fresh long red chillies, sliced thinly
350g (11 ounces) wombok (napa cabbage),
    chopped coarsely
150g (5 ounces) sugar snap peas, trimmed
¼ cup (60ml) black bean sauce
¼ cup (60ml) kecap manis
1 tablespoon rice vinegar
¼ cup (80ml) beef stock
4 green onions (scallions), sliced thinly

1   Place noodles in large heatproof bowl, cover with boiling water; stand until just tender, drain.
2   Meanwhile, heat oil in wok; stir-fry beef, onion and chilli until beef is cooked through.
3   Add wombok and peas; stir-fry until wombok is tender.
4   Add noodles and combined remaining ingredients; stir-fry until hot.

prep & cook time 30 minutes serves 4
nutritional count per serving 16.4g total fat
(6.4g saturated fat); 1559kJ (373 cal);
19.2g carbohydrate; 35.2g protein; 3.3g fibre
note You can buy jars of black bean and garlic sauce from supermarkets and Asian food shops.

stir-fried turkey with lemon & chilli

500g (1 pound) turkey breast fillets, sliced thinly
2 teaspoons finely grated lemon rind
2 fresh small red thai (serrano) chillies, chopped finely
2 teaspoons olive oil
2 cloves garlic, crushed
1 x 10cm (4 inch) stalk fresh lemon grass (20g),
   chopped finely
1 large brown onion (200g), sliced thinly
600g (1¼ pounds) fresh ramen noodles
300g (10 ounces) baby buk choy, chopped coarsely
2 tablespoons black bean sauce
¼ cup (60ml) plum sauce
¾ cup (180ml) chicken stock

1 Combine turkey, rind and chilli in medium bowl.
Heat 1 teaspoon of the oil in wok; stir-fry turkey mixture,
in batches, until browned and cooked through. Remove
from wok.
2 Heat remaining oil in wok; stir-fry garlic, lemon grass
and onion until onion is soft. Add noodles and buk choy;
stir-fry until buk choy is just wilted.
3 Return turkey to wok with sauces and stock; stir-fry
until sauce boils and thickens slightly.

prep & cook time 30 minutes **serves** 4
nutritional count per serving 8.8g total fat
(2.3g saturated fat); 1956kJ (468 cal);
54.8g carbohydrate; 39.2g protein; 5g fibre

satay pork & noodle stir-fry

500g (1 pound) fresh egg noodles
1 tablespoon vegetable oil
500g (1 pound) pork fillet, sliced thinly
2 cloves garlic, crushed
8 green onions (scallions), sliced thinly
¾ cup (180ml) beef stock
⅓ cup (85g) crunchy peanut butter
¼ cup (60ml) sweet chilli sauce
2 teaspoons lemon juice
400g (13 ounce) packet fresh asian-style
    stir-fry vegetables

1   Place noodles in large heatproof bowl, cover with
boiling water; stand until just tender, drain.
2   Heat half the oil in wok; stir-fry pork, in batches, until
browned. Remove from wok. Heat remaining oil in wok,
add garlic and onion; stir-fry until soft.
3   Add stock, peanut butter, sauce and juice; simmer,
uncovered, 1 minute. Return pork to wok with vegetables
and noodles; stir-fry until hot.

prep & cook time 30 minutes serves 4
nutritional count per serving 18.3g total fat
(3.1g saturated fat); 2257kJ (540 cal);
44.3g carbohydrate; 43g protein; 12.2g fibre

pizzas

pepperoni pizza

30cm (12 inch) purchased pizza base
⅓ cup (90g) tomato paste
2 teaspoons dried oregano
2 cups (200g) coarsely grated mozzarella cheese
¼ cup (20g) coarsely grated parmesan cheese
150g (5 ounces) thinly sliced pepperoni
½ cup (80g) seeded black olives

1 Preheat oven to 180°C/350°F.
2 Place pizza base on oiled oven tray. Spread base with combined tomato paste and oregano; sprinkle with two-thirds of the combined cheeses. Top with pepperoni and olives then remaining cheeses.
3 Bake about 20 minutes or until base is cooked through and cheese is bubbling.

prep & cook time 30 minutes **serves** 4
nutritional count per serving 31.4g total fat (13.5g saturated fat); 3064kJ (733 cal); 73.7g carbohydrate; 35.5g protein; 5.8g fibre
note Any salami, cabanossi or ham can be substituted for the pepperoni.

tomato & onion pitta pizzas

4 wholemeal pitta breads (320g)
¼ cup (60ml) bottled tomato pasta sauce
1 cup (125g) coarsely grated cheddar cheese
2 medium tomatoes (380g), sliced thinly
1 medium brown onion (150g), sliced thinly
¼ cup (30g) seeded black olives, halved

1 Preheat oven to 200°C/400°F.
2 Place pittas on lightly oiled oven trays. Spread each pitta with pasta sauce; top with half the cheese then tomato, onion and olives; sprinkle with remaining cheese.
3 Bake pizzas about 15 minutes or until browned lightly.

prep & cook time 30 minutes serves 4
nutritional count per serving 12.8g total fat
(7.1g saturated fat); 1580kJ (378 cal);
45.2g carbohydrate; 16.6g protein; 7.2g fibre

pizza with prosciutto & ricotta

3 medium egg (plum) tomatoes (225g)
3 x 25cm (10 inch) purchased pizza bases
½ cup (140g) tomato paste
300g (10 ounces) baby spinach
1 large red onion (300g), sliced thinly
9 slices prosciutto (135g), halved
¼ cup loosely packed, coarsely chopped fresh basil
1½ cups (300g) ricotta cheese
¼ cup (40g) pine nuts
¼ cup (60ml) olive oil
2 cloves garlic, crushed

1   Preheat oven to 220°C/425°F.
2   Cut each tomato into eight wedges.
3   Place pizza bases on oven trays. Spread each base with a third of the tomato paste; top with equal amounts of tomato, spinach, onion, prosciutto, basil, cheese and pine nuts. Drizzle each pizza with equal amounts of combined oil and garlic.
4   Bake about 15 minutes or until pizza tops are browned lightly and bases are crisp.

prep & cook time 30 minutes serves 6
nutritional count per serving 25.4g total fat
(6.2g saturated fat); 2562kJ (613 cal);
68.2g carbohydrate; 23.6g protein; 8.2g fibre

salami, mushroom & oregano pizza

30cm (12 inch) purchased pizza base
¼ cup (70g) tomato paste
2 teaspoons dried oregano
⅓ cup (80ml) bottled tomato pasta sauce
½ cup (150g) coarsely chopped cooked silver beet
(swiss chard)
50g (1¾ ounces) button mushrooms, sliced thinly
100g (3½ ounces) thinly sliced salami
¾ cup (75g) coarsely grated mozzarella cheese

1 Preheat oven to 180°C/350°F.
2 Place pizza base on lightly oiled oven tray. Spread combined tomato paste and oregano over base. Top with pasta sauce, silver beet, mushrooms then salami. Sprinkle with cheese.
3 Bake about 20 minutes or until base is crisp and cheese is bubbling.

prep & cook time 35 minutes **serves** 4
nutritional count per serving 18.7g total fat
(6.4g saturated fat); 2366kJ (566 cal);
71g carbohydrate; 24g protein; 8.4g fibre
tips Split a purchased base in half for a thin crust pizza. Use cut-side up and bake about 5 minutes less than the time stated.
Use your choice of mild or hot salami for this pizza.

pesto, mozzarella & artichoke pizza

30cm (12 inch) purchased pizza base
¾ cup (190g) basil pesto
100g (3½ ounces) marinated eggplant slices
200g (6½ ounces) char-grilled capsicum slices
2 drained marinated artichoke hearts, sliced thickly
200g (6½ ounces) mozzarella cheese, sliced thickly
2 tablespoons pine nuts

1 Preheat oven to 180°C/350°F.
2 Place pizza base on oiled oven tray. Spread pesto over base; top with eggplant, capsicum, artichoke then cheese. Sprinkle with nuts.
3 Bake about 20 minutes or until base is crisp and cheese is bubbling.

prep & cook time 35 minutes serves 4
nutritional count per serving 42.2g total fat (12.6g saturated fat); 3348kJ (801 cal); 70.3g carbohydrate; 31.4g protein; 8.1g fibre
note The same amount of ingredients used to top this 30cm pizza will also top four mini pizza bases.

salami & rocket pizza

2 x 25cm (10 inch) pizza bases
⅔ cup (160ml) bottled tomato pasta sauce
250g (8 ounces) mozzarella cheese, sliced thinly
125g (4 ounces) salami, sliced thinly
50g (1¾ ounces) baby rocket leaves (arugula)

1 Preheat oven to 200°C/400°F.
2 Place pizza bases on oven trays. Spread sauce evenly over bases; top with cheese and salami. Bake about 15 minutes or until cheese melts and bases are crisp.
3 Just before serving, top pizzas with rocket.

prep & cook time 25 minutes serves 4
nutritional count per serving 30.3g total fat (13.3g saturated fat); 2855kJ (683 cal); 65.9g carbohydrate; 34.3g protein; 5.2g fibre

mushroom pizza

4 x 15cm (6 inch) pizza bases
1½ cups (185g) grated pizza cheese
150g (5 ounces) flat mushrooms, sliced thinly
100g (3½ ounces) fetta cheese, crumbled
2 tablespoons finely chopped fresh chives

1 Preheat oven to 200°C/400°F.
2 Place pizza bases on oven trays. Sprinkle half the pizza cheese over bases. Divide mushroom, fetta, chives and remaining pizza cheese among bases.
3 Bake about 15 minutes or until pizza tops are browned lightly and bases are crisp.

prep & cook time 25 minutes serves 4
nutritional count per serving 25.6g total fat (11.6g saturated fat); 3988kJ (954 cal); 133.2g carbohydrate; 41.7g protein; 10.2g fibre
note We used a greek fetta, which crumbles well and has a sharp taste.

pasta

scallops with asparagus

375g (12 ounces) large pasta spirals
2 teaspoons olive oil
500g (1 pound) asparagus, trimmed, cut into
    5cm (2 inch) lengths
400g (13 ounces) scallops
1 cup (250ml) dry white wine
1¼ cups (300ml) pouring cream
2 tablespoons fresh dill tips
1 tablespoon finely shredded lemon rind
1 tablespoon lemon juice

1 Cook pasta in large saucepan of boiling water until just tender; drain.
2 Meanwhile, heat half the oil in large frying pan; cook asparagus, in batches, stirring, until just tender. Remove from pan.
3 Heat remaining oil in pan; cook scallops, in batches, until browned both sides. Remove from pan. Add wine to pan; bring to the boil; boil, uncovered, until liquid is reduced by three-quarters. Reduce heat, add cream; simmer, uncovered, until sauce thickens slightly.
4 Place pasta in pan with asparagus, scallops and remaining ingredients; toss gently over low heat until heated through.

prep & cook time 25 minutes serves 4
nutritional count per serving 36.1g total fat (22g saturated fat); 3010kJ (720 cal); 67.9g carbohydrate; 18.6g protein; 4.5g fibre

fresh tomato & caper salsa with penne

375g (12 ounces) penne pasta
6 medium tomatoes (1kg), deseeded, chopped finely
⅓ cup (80g) rinsed, drained capers, chopped coarsely
1 medium red onion (170g), chopped finely
12 basil leaves, torn
12 purple basil leaves, torn
½ cup (80g) roasted pine nuts
balsamic vinaigrette
2 cloves garlic, crushed
⅓ cup (80ml) balsamic vinegar
⅔ cup (160ml) olive oil

1 Cook pasta in large saucepan of boiling water until just tender; drain. Rinse until cold water; drain.
2 Meanwhile, make balsamic vinaigrette.
3 Place pasta in large bowl with remaining ingredients; drizzle with balsamic vinaigrette, toss gently.
balsamic vinaigrette Combine ingredients in screw-top jar; shake well.

prep & cook time 25 minutes serves 4
nutritional count per serving 51.7g total fat (6.2g saturated fat); 3436kJ (822 cal); 71g carbohydrate; 15g protein; 6.5g fibre

spaghetti with baked ricotta

375g (12 ounces) spaghetti
540g (18 ounces) bottled marinated eggplant in oil
2 cloves garlic, crushed
800g (28 ounces) canned crushed tomatoes
½ teaspoon cracked black pepper
300g (10 ounces) baked ricotta, chopped coarsely

1 Cook pasta in large saucepan of boiling water until just tender; drain.
2 Meanwhile, cook undrained eggplant and garlic in large saucepan, stirring, until fragrant.
3 Stir pasta, undrained tomatoes and pepper into eggplant mixture; toss over medium heat until combined, then gently stir in cheese.

prep & cook time 20 minutes serves 4
nutritional count per serving 33.3g total fat (9.4g saturated fat); 2955kJ (707 cal); 75.4g carbohydrate; 21.7g protein; 9.1g fibre
note You can use any kind of marinated vegetables (mushrooms, capsicums or mixed antipasti) in this recipe instead of the eggplant.

macaroni cheese

250g (8 ounces) macaroni pasta
60g (2 ounces) butter
⅓ cup (50g) plain (all-purpose) flour
3 cups (750ml) milk
2 cups (250g) coarsely grated pizza cheese

1   Cook pasta in large saucepan of boiling water until just tender; drain.
2   Meanwhile, melt butter in medium saucepan, add flour; cook, stirring, about 2 minutes or until mixture thickens and bubbles. Gradually stir in milk; cook, stirring, until sauce boils and thickens.
3   Preheat grill (broiler) to hot.
4   Stir pasta and half the cheese into sauce; pour mixture into shallow 2-litre (8-cup) baking dish. Sprinkle with remaining cheese; grill until cheese melts and is browned lightly.

prep & cook time 25 minutes **serves** 4
nutritional count per serving 34.2g total fat (21.8g saturated fat); 2863kJ (685 cal); 60.9g carbohydrate; 32.8g protein; 2.5g fibre
note This quick version doesn't have to go into the oven like the traditional macaroni cheese recipe, so it's great when you want dinner on the table fast.

fettuccine carbonara

375g (12 ounces) fettuccine pasta
4 rindless bacon slices (260g), chopped coarsely
3 egg yolks, beaten lightly
1 cup (250ml) pouring cream
½ cup (30g) finely grated parmesan cheese
2 tablespoons coarsely chopped fresh chives

1   Cook pasta in large saucepan of boiling water until just tender; drain.
2   Meanwhile, cook bacon in heated oiled small frying pan, stirring, until crisp; drain.
3   Combine pasta in large bowl with egg yolks, cream cheese and bacon; sprinkle with chives.

prep & cook time 20 minutes **serves** 4
nutritional count per serving 39.8g total fat (22.8g saturated fat); 3122kJ (747 cal); 66.1g carbohydrate; 29.8g protein; 3.1g fibre
note Try pancetta or prosciutto instead of the bacon.

fettuccine alfredo

375g (12 ounces) fettuccine pasta
2 teaspoons olive oil
4 green onions (scallions), sliced thinly
1 clove garlic, crushed
2 tablespoons dry white wine
1¼ cups (300ml) pouring cream
1 teaspoon dijon mustard
¼ cup loosely packed, finely chopped fresh
   flat-leaf parsley
1 cup (80g) finely grated parmesan cheese

1   Cook pasta in large saucepan of boiling water until just tender; drain.
2   Meanwhile, heat oil in medium saucepan; cook onion and garlic, stirring, until onion softens. Add wine and cream; bring to the boil. Reduce heat; simmer, stirring, about 2 minutes or until sauce is smooth. Stir in mustard.
3   Add pasta, parsley and cheese to sauce; toss gently.

prep & cook time 30 minutes serves 4
nutritional count per serving 42.3g total fat
(26.1g saturated fat); 3076kJ (736 cal);
66.4g carbohydrate; 19.8g protein; 3.5g fibre

roasted kumara
& parmesan pasta

1 large kumara (orange sweet potato) (500g)
2 tablespoons olive oil
250g (8 ounces) curly lasagne pasta
1 cup (80g) shaved parmesan cheese
250g (8 ounces) rocket leaves (arugula), torn
¼ cup (60ml) balsamic vinegar
¼ cup (60ml) olive oil, extra
1 clove garlic, crushed

1   Preheat oven to 220°C/425°F.
2   Halve kumara lengthways; slice halves into 5mm (¼ inch) pieces. Combine kumara with oil in large baking dish; roast, uncovered, about 25 minutes or until tender.
3   Meanwhile, break lasagne roughly lengthways, cook in large saucepan of boiling water until just tender; drain.
4   Place pasta, kumara, cheese, rocket and combined remaining ingredients in large bowl; toss gently.

prep & cook time 35 minutes serves 4
nutritional count per serving 30.5g total fat
(7.5g saturated fat); 2487kJ (595 cal);
59.1g carbohydrate; 18.3g protein; 5g fibre
note In this recipe we used broken curly lasagne, sometimes called pappardelle or lasagnette, but you can substitute any shape pasta you like.

gnocchi al quattro formaggi

¼ cup (60ml) dry white wine
1 cup (250g) mascarpone cheese
1 cup (120g) coarsely grated mozzarella cheese
½ cup (40g) coarsely grated parmesan cheese
¼ cup (60ml) milk
625g (1¼ pounds) potato gnocchi
75g (2½ ounces) gorgonzola cheese, crumbled

1   Add wine to large saucepan; boil, uncovered, until wine reduces by half. Reduce heat, add mascarpone; stir until mixture is smooth. Add mozzarella, parmesan and milk; cook, stirring, until cheeses melt and sauce is smooth in consistency.
2   Meanwhile, cook gnocchi in large saucepan of boiling water until gnocchi rise to the surface and are just tender; drain.
3   Add gnocchi and gorgonzola to sauce; toss gently.

prep & cook time 20 minutes serves 4
nutritional count per serving 53.7g total fat (34.1g saturated fat); 3256kJ (779 cal); 47.4g carbohydrate; 23.3g protein; 3.6g fibre
note If this pasta dish, with its sauce of four cheeses, is served as a first course, try not to follow it with a main course that's equally rich. Grilled plain chops or poached fish fillets are perfect possibilities.

spaghetti with chilli & leek

375g (12 ounces) spaghetti
4 rindless bacon slices (260g), chopped coarsely
80g (2¾ ounces) butter
2 small leeks (400g), sliced thinly
2 cloves garlic, crushed
2 fresh small red thai (serrano) chillies, chopped finely
6 green onions (scallions), chopped finely
½ cup (40g) finely grated parmesan cheese

1   Cook pasta in large saucepan of boiling water until just tender; drain.
2   Meanwhile, cook bacon in heated oiled medium frying pan until browned; drain on absorbent paper.
3   Melt butter in same pan; cook leek and garlic, stirring, about 5 minutes or until leek softens. Add bacon, chilli and onion; cook, stirring, 2 minutes or until onion is soft.
4   Place pasta in large bowl with leek mixture and cheese; toss gently.

prep & cook time 25 minutes serves 4
nutritional count per serving 26.7g total fat (15.2g saturated fat); 2663kJ (637 cal); 67.2g carbohydrate; 29.2g protein; 5.4g fibre

fettuccine alle vongole

375g (12 ounces) fettuccine pasta
2 tablespoons olive oil
3 cloves garlic, crushed
1 fresh long red chilli, chopped finely
1 tablespoon rinsed, drained baby capers
¾ cup (180ml) dry white wine
¾ cup (180ml) fish stock
2 tablespoons lemon juice
1kg (2 pounds) clams
½ cup coarsely chopped fresh flat-leaf parsley
¼ cup coarsely chopped fresh chives

1 Cook pasta in large saucepan of boiling water until just tender; drain.
2 To make vongole mixture, heat oil in large saucepan; cook garlic and chilli, stirring, 1 minute. Add capers, wine, stock and juice; bring to the boil. Add clams; cook vongole mixture, covered, about 5 minutes or until clams open (discard any that do not).
3 Add pasta and herbs to vongole mixture; toss gently.

prep & cook time 30 minutes serves 4
nutritional count per serving 10.5g total fat
(1.6g saturated fat); 2019kJ (483 cal);
66.1g carbohydrate; 20.4g protein; 4.2g fibre
note A classic pasta vongole is made with tiny baby clams in Italy, but you can use a mixture of any available bivalves for this recipe.

roasted capsicum, goat's cheese & walnut salad

375g (12 ounces) large pasta spirals
2 medium red capsicums (bell pepper) (400g)
2 medium yellow capsicums (bell pepper) (400g)
150g (5 ounces) goat's cheese, crumbled
⅓ cup (35g) walnuts, roasted, chopped coarsely
½ cup loosely packed fresh basil leaves
¼ cup (60ml) red wine vinegar
⅓ cup (80ml) olive oil
1 clove garlic, crushed
2 teaspoons wholegrain mustard

1 Cook pasta in large saucepan of boiling water until just tender; drain. Rinse under cold water; drain.
2 Meanwhile, preheat grill (broiler).
3 Quarter capsicums, remove and discard seeds and membranes. Roast under hot grill, skin-side up, until skin blisters and blackens. Cover capsicum pieces with plastic or paper for 5 minutes, peel away skin then slice capsicum thickly.
4 Place pasta and capsicum in large bowl with cheese, walnuts, basil and combined remaining ingredients; toss gently.

prep & cook time 30 minutes **serves** 4
nutritional count per serving 31.6g total fat (7g saturated fat); 2771kJ (663 cal); 71.5g carbohydrate; 19.6g protein; 5.9g fibre
notes Fetta or any soft, crumbly cheese can be used instead of the goat's cheese.
Roasted pecan halves can be used instead of walnuts.

fettuccine with rocket pesto & fresh tomato salsa

500g (1 pound) fettuccine pasta
8 cloves garlic, quartered
½ cup coarsely chopped fresh basil
120g (4 ounces) rocket (arugula), chopped coarsely
⅔ cup (160ml) olive oil
½ cup (40g) finely grated parmesan cheese
3 medium tomatoes (570g), chopped coarsely
2 tablespoons lemon juice
2 fresh small red thai (serrano) chillies, sliced thinly
⅓ cup (50g) pine nuts, roasted

1   Cook pasta in large saucepan of boiling water until just tender; drain.
2   Meanwhile, to make rocket pesto, blend or process garlic, basil, rocket and oil until smooth.
3   Combine pasta, rocket pesto, cheese, tomato, juice and chilli in large saucepan; cook, stirring, until hot. Add nuts; toss gently.

prep & cook time 25 minutes serves 4
nutritional count per serving 50.3g total fat (8g saturated fat); 3846kJ (920 cal); 90.3g carbohydrate; 22.2g protein; 8.2g fibre
note For a milder pesto, substitute baby spinach leaves for the rocket.

pasta with peas & prosciutto

1 tablespoon olive oil
1 large brown onion (200g), sliced thickly
1 clove garlic, crushed
6 slices prosciutto (100g), chopped coarsely
2⅓ cups (600ml) bottled tomato pasta sauce
½ cup (125ml) pouring cream
2 cups (250g) frozen peas
250g (8 ounces) curly lasagne pasta

1   Heat oil in large saucepan; cook onion, garlic and prosciutto, stirring, until onion softens. Add sauce, cream and peas; bring to the boil. Reduce heat; simmer, uncovered, until sauce thickens slightly.
2   Meanwhile, cook pasta in large saucepan of boiling water until just tender; drain.
3   Place pasta in large bowl with sauce; toss gently.

prep & cook time 20 minutes serves 4
nutritional count per serving 21.7g total fat
(10.4g saturated fat); 2303kJ (551 cal);
65.8g carbohydrate; 18.8g protein; 10.4g fibre

mixed mushroom orecchiette

1 tablespoon olive oil
1 medium brown onion (150g), chopped finely
2 cloves garlic, crushed
250g (8 ounces) button mushrooms, sliced thickly
250g (8 ounces) swiss brown mushrooms, sliced thickly
250g (8 ounces) flat mushrooms, sliced thickly
250g (8 ounces) spreadable cream cheese
½ cup (125ml) chicken stock
375g (12 ounces) orecchiette pasta
½ teaspoon cracked black pepper
2 tablespoons coarsely chopped fresh flat-leaf parsley

1   Heat oil in large frying pan; cook onion and garlic, stirring, until onion softens. Add mushrooms; cook, stirring, until browned and tender. Add cream cheese and stock; cook, stirring, over low heat, until cheese melts and mixture is hot.
2   Meanwhile, cook pasta in large saucepan of boiling water until just tender; drain. Stir pasta into mushroom sauce; stir in pepper and parsley.

prep & cook time 25 minutes serves 4
nutritional count per serving 27g total fat
(14.2g saturated fat); 2667kJ (638 cal);
70.8g carbohydrate; 23.6g protein; 8.6g fibre

risoni with spinach & semi-dried tomatoes

30g (1 ounce) butter
2 medium brown onions (300g), chopped finely
3 cloves garlic, crushed
500g (1 pound) risoni pasta
4 cups (1 litre) chicken stock
½ cup (125ml) dry white wine
150g (5 ounces) semi-dried tomatoes, halved
100g (3½ ounces) baby spinach leaves
⅓ cup (25g) finely grated parmesan cheese

1   Melt butter in large saucepan; cook onion and garlic, stirring, until onion softens. Add risoni; stir to coat in butter mixture. Stir in stock and wine; bring to the boil. Reduce heat; simmer over medium heat, stirring, until liquid is absorbed and risoni is just tender.
2   Gently stir in tomato, spinach and cheese.

prep & cook time 30 minutes **serves** 4
nutritional count per serving 13.7g total fat (6.5g saturated fat); 2880kJ (689 cal); 104.4g carbohydrate; 25.2g protein; 10.8g fibre
note Risoni is a small pasta shaped like a grain of rice. You can substitute any small pasta in this recipe.

tagliatelle puttanesca

2 teaspoons vegetable oil
1 large brown onion (200g), sliced thickly
3 cloves garlic, crushed
4 fresh small red thai (serrano) chillies, chopped finely
2⅓ cups (600ml) bottled tomato pasta sauce
¼ cup (40g) rinsed, drained capers
1 cup (160g) seeded kalamata olives
8 drained anchovy fillets, halved
½ cup coarsely chopped fresh flat-leaf parsley
375g (12 ounces) tagliatelle pasta

1   Heat oil in large frying pan; cook onion, garlic and chilli, stirring, until onion softens. Add sauce, capers, olives and anchovies; bring to the boil. Reduce heat; simmer, uncovered, about 5 minutes or until sauce thickens slightly. Stir in parsley.
2   Meanwhile, cook pasta in large saucepan of boiling water until just tender; drain. Serve pasta with sauce.

prep & cook time 30 minutes **serves** 4
nutritional count per serving 9.4g total fat (1.8g saturated fat); 2529kJ (605 cal); 104g carbohydrate; 20.6g protein; 9g fibre

rigatoni with eggplant sauce

¼ cup (60ml) olive oil
1 medium brown onion (150g), chopped finely
2 stalks celery (300g), trimmed, chopped finely
1 clove garlic, crushed
2 tablespoons brandy
1 medium eggplant (300g), sliced thinly
2⅓ cups (600ml) bottled tomato pasta sauce
½ cup (140g) tomato paste
½ cup (125ml) water
375g (12 ounces) rigatoni pasta
¼ cup (20g) finely grated parmesan cheese

1 Heat oil in large saucepan; cook onion, celery and garlic, stirring, until onion softens. Add brandy; cook, stirring, until brandy evaporates. Add eggplant; cook, stirring, until eggplant is tender.
2 Stir in sauce, paste and the water; bring to the boil. Reduce heat; simmer, uncovered, about 10 minutes or until sauce thickens slightly.
3 Meanwhile, cook pasta in large saucepan of boiling water until just tender; drain.
4 Place pasta in large bowl with half the eggplant sauce; toss gently. Divide pasta among serving plates; top with remaining sauce then cheese.

prep & cook time 30 minutes serves 4
nutritional count per serving 21.5g total fat
(4.2g saturated fat); 3031kJ (725 cal);
100g carbohydrate; 21.8g protein; 11.4g fibre

orecchiette with artichokes, ham & sun-dried tomatoes

375g (12 ounces) orecchiette pasta
340g (11 ounces) bottled artichoke hearts in oil, drained, quartered
½ cup (75g) sun-dried tomatoes, halved
1 cup (80g) flaked parmesan cheese
1 cup loosely packed fresh flat-leaf parsley leaves
500g (1 pound) ham, sliced thickly
2 tablespoons lemon juice
1 tablespoon wholegrain mustard
1 tablespoon honey
1 clove garlic, crushed
½ cup (125ml) olive oil

1 Cook pasta in large saucepan of boiling water until just tender; drain.
2 Place pasta in large bowl with artichokes, tomato, cheese, parsley, ham and combined remaining ingredients; toss gently.

prep & cook time 25 minutes **serves** 4
nutritional count per serving 46.6g total fat (11.5g saturated fat); 3896kJ (932 cal); 78g carbohydrate; 46.2g protein; 7.5g fibre
note If you can find fresh orecchiette (little ears), use them instead of the packaged dried version.

greek lamb, fetta & eggplant pasta

1 medium eggplant (300g), chopped coarsely
cooking (kosher) salt
500g (1 pound) lamb fillets
2 tablespoons olive oil
250g (8 ounces) large pasta shells
1 medium red onion (170g), sliced thinly
100g (3½ ounces) baby rocket (arugula) leaves
2 medium tomatoes (380g), deseeded, sliced thinly
¼ cup loosely packed fresh oregano leaves
200g (6½ ounces) fetta cheese, crumbled
balsamic vinaigrette
¼ cup (60ml) balsamic vinegar
½ cup (125ml) olive oil
2 cloves garlic, crushed
2 tablespoons wholegrain mustard

1 Place eggplant in colander, sprinkle all over with salt. Stand 5 minutes; rinse under cold water, drain on absorbent paper.
2 Meanwhile, cook lamb, in batches, in heated oiled large frying pan until browned and cooked as desired. Cover; stand 5 minutes then cut into thick slices.
3 Heat oil in same pan; cook eggplant, in batches, until browned all over and tender.
4 Meanwhile, cook pasta in large saucepan of boiling water until just tender; drain.
5 Make vinaigrette.
6 Place pasta, lamb and eggplant in large bowl with remaining ingredients; drizzle with balsamic vinaigrette, toss gently.
balsamic vinaigrette Combine ingredients in screw-top jar; shake well.

prep & cook time 35 minutes serves 4
nutritional count per serving 56.4g total fat
(15.1g saturated fat); 3749kJ (897 cal);
48.8g carbohydrate; 46g protein; 5.7g fibre

chicken & fennel spirals

2 medium fennel bulbs (1kg), trimmed, sliced thinly
3 cloves garlic, sliced thinly
¼ cup (60ml) dry sherry
1½ cups (375ml) chicken stock
375g (12 ounces) large pasta spirals
2 cups (340g) shredded cooked chicken
200g (6½ ounces) snow peas, trimmed, sliced thinly
1 cup (240g) sour cream
1 tablespoon coarsely chopped fresh tarragon

1 Preheat oven to 220°C/425°F.
2 Combine fennel, garlic, sherry and ½ cup of the stock in large baking dish; roast, uncovered, about 15 minutes or until fennel is just tender.
3 Meanwhile, cook pasta in large saucepan of boiling water until just tender; drain.
4 Return pasta to same pan with fennel mixture, remaining stock and remaining ingredients; stir over low heat until hot.

prep & cook time 30 minutes **serves** 4
nutritional count per serving 32g total fat
(17.9g saturated fat); 3189kJ (763 cal);
73.6g carbohydrate; 36.8g protein; 8.6g fibre

chicken liver sauce with curly lasagne

500g (1 pound) chicken livers
½ cup (50g) packaged breadcrumbs
¼ cup (60ml) olive oil
1 medium brown onion (150g), chopped coarsely
4 medium tomatoes (520g), chopped coarsely
½ cup (125ml) chicken stock
¼ cup (60ml) balsamic vinegar
¼ cup (60ml) dry red wine
2 tablespoons coarsely chopped fresh rosemary
375g (12 ounces) curly lasagne pasta

1 Halve each trimmed chicken liver lobe; toss in breadcrumbs, shaking off excess. Heat half the oil in large frying pan; cook liver, over high heat, in batches, until browned and cooked (see note, below). Remove from pan.

2 Heat remaining oil in same pan; cook onion, stirring, until soft. Add tomato; cook, stirring, until tomato is pulpy. Add stock, vinegar, wine and rosemary to pan; cook, stirring, until sauce thickens slightly.

3 Meanwhile, cook pasta in large saucepan of boiling water until just tender; drain.

4 Stir pasta and liver into tomato sauce.

prep & cook time 30 minutes serves 4
nutritional count per serving 20.3g total fat
(3.9g saturated fat); 2801kJ (670 cal);
78.2g carbohydrate; 36.9g protein; 5.7g fibre
note Be sure not to overcook the chicken livers or they will be dry and unappealing.

seafood

moroccan fish fillets with fruity couscous

1 clove garlic, crushed
1cm (½ inch) piece fresh ginger (5g), grated finely
1 teaspoon ground cumin
½ teaspoon ground turmeric
½ teaspoon hot paprika
½ teaspoon ground coriander
4 firm white fish fillets (800g), skin removed
1 tablespoon olive oil

fruity couscous

2 cups (400g) couscous
2 cups (500ml) boiling water
50g (1¾ ounces) butter
1 large pear (330g), chopped finely
½ cup (75g) finely chopped dried apricots
½ cup (95g) coarsely chopped dried figs
½ cup coarsely chopped fresh flat-leaf parsley
¼ cup (40g) roasted pine nuts

1 Combine garlic, ginger and spices in large bowl, add fish; toss to coat fish in spice mixture. Heat oil in large frying pan; cook fish, in batches, until browned both sides and cooked as desired.
2 Meanwhile, make fruity couscous.
3 Divide couscous among serving plates; top with fish. Accompany with a bowl of combined yogurt and coarsely chopped fresh coriander, if desired.

fruity couscous Combine couscous, the water and butter in large heatproof bowl, cover; stand about 5 minutes or until liquid is absorbed, fluffing with fork occasionally. Stir in remaining ingredients.

prep & cook time 35 minutes serves 4
nutritional count per serving 27.1g total fat (9.3g saturated fat); 3821kJ (914 cal); 106.5g carbohydrate; 57g protein; 8.5 g fibre

fish milanese

1 small brown onion (80g), chopped finely
2 tablespoons lemon juice
⅓ cup (80ml) olive oil
4 firm white fish fillets (800g)
⅓ cup (50g) plain (all-purpose) flour
2 eggs, beaten lightly
1 tablespoon milk
1 cup (100g) packaged breadcrumbs
1 tablespoon olive oil, extra
120g (4 ounces) butter
1 clove garlic, crushed
2 teaspoons finely chopped fresh flat-leaf parsley

1   Combine onion, juice and oil in medium shallow bowl, add fish; spoon mixture over fish to coat thoroughly. Cover; refrigerate 1 hour, turning occasionally.
2   Remove fish from marinade. Coat lightly with flour; shake away excess. Combine egg and milk in small bowl; dip fish into egg mixture then coat in breadcrumbs, press on firmly.
3   Heat extra oil and half of the butter in large frying pan. Cook fish, about 3 minutes each side, or until cooked through; drain on absorbent paper.
4   Heat remaining butter in small saucepan. Cook garlic until butter turns a light golden brown; add parsley. Pour browned butter over fish.

prep & cook time 30 minutes (+ refrigeration) **serves** 4
nutritional count per serving 56g total fat
(22.1g saturated fat); 3398kJ (813 cal);
27.4g carbohydrate; 50.1g protein; 1.9g fibre

crumbed calamari rings

1 egg
2 tablespoons milk
1kg (2 pounds) calamari rings, sliced thinly
2 cups (200g) packaged breadcrumbs
vegetable oil for deep-frying

1   Beat egg and milk in small bowl. Dip calamari in egg mixture; drain away excess. Toss in breadcrumbs; press breadcrumbs on firmly.
2   Heat oil in large saucepan. Deep-fry calamari, in batches, about 2 minutes or until golden brown; drain on absorbent paper. Serve with lemon wedges and tartare sauce, if you like.

prep & cook time 30 minutes serves 4
nutritional count per serving 20.4g total fat
(3.8g saturated fat); 2199kJ (526 cal);
33.4g carbohydrate; 50.8g protein; 2.1g fibre
notes Two cloves of crushed garlic can be added to the egg mixture.
Calamari can be shallow-fried. Heat a small amount of oil in a large frying pan; the oil should only reach halfway up the side of each calamari ring. Cook calamari rings in hot oil, about 2 minutes each side, or until golden brown.

grilled snapper fillets
with fennel & onion salad

1 medium red onion (170g), sliced thinly
4 green onions (scallions), sliced thinly
1 large fennel bulb (550g), trimmed, sliced thinly
2 stalks celery (300g), trimmed, sliced thinly
½ cup coarsely chopped fresh flat-leaf parsley
⅓ cup (80ml) orange juice
¼ cup (60ml) olive oil
2 cloves garlic, crushed
2 teaspoons sambal oelek
4 snapper fillets (1kg), skin on

1 Combine both onions, fennel, celery and parsley in medium bowl.
2 Place juice, oil, garlic and sambal in screw-top jar; shake well.
3 Cook fish on heated oiled grill plate (or grill or barbecue) until browned both sides and cooked as desired.
4 Pour half the dressing over salad in bowl; toss gently. Serve salad topped with fish; drizzle with remaining dressing.

prep & cook time 25 minutes **serves** 4
nutritional count per serving 18.4g total fat (3.6g saturated fat); 1839kJ (440 cal); 8.2g carbohydrate; 57.9g protein; 4.5g fibre

sardines with tomatoes & caper dressing

16 fresh sardines (750g), cleaned
4 medium egg (plum) tomatoes (300g), sliced thickly
1 small red onion (100g), sliced thinly
1 tablespoon coarsely chopped fresh flat-leaf parsley
caper dressing
⅓ cup (80ml) red wine vinegar
¼ cup (60ml) extra virgin olive oil
1 tablespoon rinsed, drained baby capers
1 clove garlic, crushed
1 tablespoon finely chopped fresh flat-leaf parsley

1 Make caper dressing.
2 To butterfly the sardines, cut through the underside to the tail. Break backbone at tail; peel away backbone. Trim sardines.
3 Cook sardines on heated, oiled grill plate (or grill or barbecue), in batches, until browned both sides and just cooked through. Serve sardines with tomato and onion; drizzle over caper dressing, top with parsley.
caper dressing Combine ingredients in screw-top jar; shake well.

prep & cook time 30 minutes serves 4
nutritional count per serving 22.8g total fat
(4g saturated fat); 1367kJ (327 cal);
3.2g carbohydrate; 26.1g protein; 1.5g fibre
note Ask your fishmonger to butterfly the sardines for you.

fish cutlets in hot & spicy marinade

4 firm white fish cutlets (1kg)
marinade
1 tablespoon paprika
2 teaspoons ground ginger
1 teaspoon curry powder
¼ teaspoon chilli powder
¼ cup (60ml) brown vinegar
¼ cup (60ml) tomato paste
1 cup (250ml) dry white wine
2 cloves garlic, crushed

1 Make marinade.
2 Combine fish and marinade in large bowl. Cover; refrigerate 3 hours or overnight.
3 Remove fish from marinade; discard marinade.
4 Cook fish on heated oiled grill plate (or grill or barbecue) until cooked as desired. Serve with couscous and lemon, if you like.
marinade Combine ingredients in medium bowl.

prep & cook time 20 minutes (+ refrigeration) serves 4
nutritional count per serving 4.5g total fat
(1.4g saturated fat); 1099kJ (263 cal);
2.2g carbohydrate; 41.6g protein; 1g fibre

pan-fried fish steaks with rosemary & oregano

4 firm white fish steaks (800g)
¼ cup (60ml) lemon juice
½ cup (125ml) extra virgin olive oil
1 teaspoon salt
2 teaspoons finely chopped fresh oregano
2 teaspoons finely chopped fresh rosemary

1   Cook fish on heated oiled grill plate (or grill or barbecue) until cooked through; turn once during cooking.
2   Meanwhile, combine remaining ingredients in screw-top jar; shake well.
3   Brush both sides of hot fish with herb dressing; serve with any remaining dressing. Accompany with patty-pan squash, if desired.

prep & cook time 15 minutes serves 4
nutritional count per serving 32.9g total fat
(5.4g saturated fat); 1923kJ (460 cal);
0.4g carbohydrate; 40.9g protein; 0g fibre

fish with garlic & chilli

¼ cup (60ml) olive oil
4 firm white fish fillets, skin on (800g)
1 clove garlic, crushed
1½ tablespoons sherry vinegar
1 teaspoon dried chilli flakes
2 tablespoons finely chopped fresh flat-leaf parsley

1   Heat 1 tablespoon of the oil in large frying pan. Cook fish, flesh-side down, until well browned. Turn fish; cook until browned and just cooked through.
2   Meanwhile, place remaining oil, garlic, vinegar, chilli and parsley in small saucepan; stir over low heat until just warm – do not overheat. Spoon oil mixture over fish. Serve with lemon wedges and steamed zucchini and beans, if desired.

prep & cook time 15 minutes serves 4
nutritional count per serving 18.1g total fat
(3.3g saturated fat); 1367kJ (327 cal);
0.1g carbohydrate; 40.9g protein; 0.2g fibre
note Sherry vinegar is available in some supermarkets; if unavailable, substitute red or white wine vinegar.

steamed scallops with asian flavours

1½ cups (300g) jasmine rice
3cm (1¼ inch) piece fresh ginger (15g)
20 scallops (800g), on the half shell, roe removed
2 tablespoons thinly sliced fresh lemon grass
4 green onions (scallions), sliced thinly
1 tablespoon sesame oil
¼ cup (60ml) kecap manis
¼ cup (60ml) japanese soy sauce

1   Cook rice in large saucepan of boiling water until just tender; drain.
2   Meanwhile, slice ginger thinly; cut slices into thin strips. Place scallops, in batches, in single layer, in large bamboo steamer; top with ginger, lemon grass and onion. Steam scallops, covered, over medium saucepan of simmering water about 5 minutes or until tender and cooked as desired.
3   Divide scallops among serving plates; top with combined remaining ingredients. Serve with rice.

prep & cook time 30 minutes serves 4
nutritional count per serving 5.5g total fat
(0.9g saturated fat); 1509kJ (361 cal);
60.8g carbohydrate; 15.5g protein; 0.7g fibre

smoked trout & crisp noodle salad

450g (14 ounces) smoked ocean trout fillets
3½ cups (280g) finely shredded red cabbage
2 medium carrots (240g), grated coarsely
200g (6½ ounces) packets crispy fried noodles
4 green onions (scallions), sliced thinly
2 tablespoons toasted sesame seeds
½ cup (125ml) sweet chilli sauce
1 tablespoon sesame oil
2 tablespoons white wine vinegar
2 tablespoons japanese soy sauce

1   Discard skin and bones from fish. Flake fish into large bowl; add cabbage, carrot, noodles, onion and seeds.
2   Place remaining ingredients in screw-top jar; shake well. Drizzle dressing over salad; toss gently.

prep time 25 minutes **serves** 4
nutritional count per serving 20.8g total fat (5.4g saturated fat); 1814kJ (434 cal); 23.1g carbohydrate; 34.8g protein; 7.1g fibre
notes Filleted portions of smoked trout, in a variety of sizes, are now available at most supermarkets; we used three 150g portions for this recipe.
Crispy fried noodles are crisp wheat noodles packaged (commonly in 100g packets) already deep-fried.
You need a quarter of a medium red cabbage, about 375g, for this recipe.

crab & apple salad

250g (8 ounces) sugar snap peas, trimmed
1 large green apple (200g), unpeeled
500g (1 pound) cooked crab meat
1 medium red onion (170g), halved, sliced thinly
2 fresh small red thai (serrano) chillies, sliced thinly
    lengthways
2 medium avocados (500g), sliced thickly
150g (5 ounces) mixed salad leaves
⅓ cup (80ml) olive oil
¼ cup (60ml) lemon juice
1 tablespoon dijon mustard
1 clove garlic, crushed

1   Boil, steam or microwave peas until just tender; drain.
Rinse under cold water; drain.
2   Slice apple thinly; cut slices into thin strips. Combine
peas and apple in large bowl with crab, onion, chilli,
avocado and salad leaves.
3   Place remaining ingredients in screw-top jar; shake
well. Drizzle dressing over salad; toss gently.

prep & cook time 25 minutes serves 4
nutritional count per serving 39.1g total fat
(6.9g saturated fat); 2082kJ (498 cal);
11.2g carbohydrate; 23.6g protein; 4.9g fibre

chicken

chicken caesar salad

4 slices white bread (180g)
2 tablespoons olive oil
4 rindless bacon slices (260g), sliced thinly
3 cups (480g) coarsely chopped barbecued chicken
1 large cos lettuce, trimmed and torn
6 green onions (scallions), sliced thinly
1 cup (80g) flaked parmesan cheese
caesar dressing
¾ cup (225g) whole-egg mayonnaise
1 tablespoon lemon juice
4 drained anchovy fillets, chopped finely
3 teaspoons dijon mustard
1 tablespoon water

1 Preheat oven to 160°C/325°F.
2 Make caesar dressing.
3 To make croûtons, remove and discard crusts from bread, cut bread into 2cm (¾ inch) squares; toss with oil in medium bowl. Place bread, in single layer, on oven tray; toast in oven, 10 minutes.
4 Cook bacon in small frying pan, stirring, until browned and crisp. Drain on absorbent paper.
5 Combine half the chicken, half the bacon, half the croûtons and half the dressing in large bowl with lettuce, half the onion and half the cheese; toss gently.
6 Divide salad among serving plates. Top with remaining chicken, bacon, croûtons, onion and cheese; drizzle with remaining dressing.
caesar dressing Blend or process ingredients until mixture is smooth.

prep & cook time 25 minutes serves 4
nutritional count per serving 53.5g total fat (13.8g saturated fat); 3595kJ (860 cal); 34.9g carbohydrate; 57.6g protein; 5.6g fibre

tandoori chicken

1 cup (280g) low-fat plain yogurt
2 tablespoons lemon juice
1cm (½ inch) piece fresh ginger (5g), grated
2 cloves garlic, crushed
1 teaspoon caster (superfine) sugar
1 teaspoon paprika
½ teaspoon ground cumin
½ teaspoon ground coriander
½ teaspoon ground turmeric
pinch chilli powder
4 chicken breast fillets (800g)

tomato and coriander salsa
2 small tomatoes (180g), chopped finely
1 small red onion (100g), chopped finely
2 teaspoons caster (superfine) sugar
2 tablespoons finely chopped fresh coriander
   (cilantro)

1   Combine yogurt, juice, ginger, garlic, sugar and spices in large bowl. Add chicken; turn to coat in marinade. Refrigerate 3 hours or overnight.
2   Cook chicken on heated oiled grill plate (or grill or barbecue), brushing with marinade, until browned both sides and tender.
3   Meanwhile, make tomato and coriander salsa.
4   Slice chicken thickly; serve with salsa, and steamed jasmine rice, if you like.
tomato and coriander salsa Combine ingredients in small bowl.

prep & cook time 25 minutes (+ refrigeration) **serves** 4
nutritional count per serving 12.3g total fat (4.2g saturated fat); 1467kJ (351 cal); 11.1g carbohydrate; 47.3g protein; 1.1g fibre

chicken tikka with cucumber mint raita

1kg (2 pounds) chicken breast fillets
½ cup (150g) tikka paste
cucumber mint raita
¾ cup (200g) plain yogurt
½ lebanese cucumber (130g), peeled, seeded, chopped finely
2 tablespoons finely chopped fresh mint
1 teaspoon ground cumin

1   Combine chicken with paste in large bowl.
2   Make cucumber mint raita.
3   Cook chicken, in batches, on heated oiled grill plate (or grill or barbecue) until browned and cooked through.
4   Slice chicken; serve with cucumber mint raita on a bed of cabbage with mango chutney, if you like.
cucumber mint raita   Combine ingredients in small bowl.

prep & cook time 25 minutes serves 4
nutritional count per serving 29g total fat (7.8g saturated fat); 2232kJ (534 cal); 7.7g carbohydrate; 58.4g protein; 4.1g fibre
notes You can also serve this recipe in the traditional manner, by threading chopped chicken breast fillets onto bamboo skewers before grilling or barbecuing. You will need to soak 12 bamboo skewers in water for at least 30 minutes before use, to prevent them from splintering and scorching during cooking, or cover the ends with foil.

chicken chilli stir-fry

500g (1 pound) chicken breast fillets, sliced thinly
3 fresh small red thai (serrano) chillies, sliced thinly
1 clove garlic, crushed
300g (10 ounces) snow peas
1 large red capsicum (bell pepper) (350g), sliced thinly
¼ cup (60ml) oyster sauce
2 tablespoons thinly sliced fresh basil leaves
1½ cups (120g) bean sprouts

1 Heat oiled wok; stir-fry chicken, in batches, until browned and tender. Remove from wok.
2 Add chilli, garlic, snow peas and capsicum to wok; stir-fry until vegetables are tender. Return chicken to wok with remaining ingredients; stir-fry until hot.

prep & cook time 30 minutes **serves** 4
nutritional count per serving 7.4g total fat
(2.2g saturated fat); 1037kJ (248 cal);
11.1g carbohydrate; 31.9g protein; 3.8g fibre

chicken & green beans with thai basil

700g (1½ pounds) green beans
1 tablespoon peanut oil
4 chicken thigh fillets (800g), chopped coarsely
2 medium white onions (300g), sliced thickly
3 cloves garlic, crushed
1 teaspoon five-spice powder
½ cup (125ml) oyster sauce
2 tablespoons light soy sauce
½ cup (75g) cashews, roasted
½ cup loosely packed thai basil leaves

1 Cut beans into 5cm (2 inch) lengths.
2 Heat half the oil in wok; stir-fry chicken, in batches, until browned and cooked through. Remove from wok.
3 Heat remaining oil in wok; stir-fry onion, garlic and five-spice until onion softens. Add beans; stir-fry until beans are tender. Return chicken to wok with sauces and nuts; stir-fry until sauce boils and thickens slightly. Remove from heat; stir in basil. Serve with noodles or steamed rice, if you like.

prep & cook time 20 minutes **serves** 4
nutritional count per serving 30.5g total fat
(7.4g saturated fat); 2399kJ (574 cal);
20.1g carbohydrate; 51g protein; 7.4g fibre
note Thai basil is available from Asian grocery stores; if unavailable, sweet basil can be substituted.

thai-style chicken & vegetable curry

2 tablespoons finely chopped lemon grass
4 kaffir lime leaves, shredded finely
1 medium leek (350g), sliced thickly
2 tablespoons thai green curry paste
500g (1 pound) chicken tenderloins, halved
750ml (24 ounces) canned low-fat evaporated milk
1 litre (4 cups) vegetable stock
2 tablespoons japanese soy sauce
4 small zucchini (360g), chopped thinly
300g (10 ounces) green beans, halved
½ small wombok (napa cabbage) (350g),
    chopped coarsely
350g (11 ounces) buk choy, chopped coarsely
200g (6½ ounces) baby spinach leaves
1½ teaspoons coconut essence
2 tablespoons lime juice
¼ cup coarsely chopped fresh coriander (cilantro)

1 Heat oiled large pan; cook lemon grass, lime leaves and leek until soft. Add paste; stir until fragrant. Add chicken; cook until browned. Stir in milk, stock and sauce; simmer about 5 minutes or until thickened slightly.
2 Add vegetables; simmer, uncovered, until vegetables are just tender. Stir in essence, juice and coriander.

prep & cook time 30 minutes serves 6
nutritional count per serving 8.8g total fat
(2.3g saturated fat); 1367kJ (327 cal);
22.2g carbohydrate; 35.9g protein; 7.9g fibre

grilled chicken with green olive butter

400g (13 ounces) baby new potatoes, sliced thickly
4 chicken breast fillets (800g)
150g (5 ounces) baby spinach leaves
green olive butter
100g (3½ ounces) butter, softened
¾ cup (90g) seeded green olives, chopped coarsely
1 teaspoon finely grated lemon rind
1 clove garlic, crushed
1 tablespoon coarsely chopped fresh basil

1 Make green olive butter.
2 Boil, steam or microwave potato until tender; drain. Cover to keep warm.
3 Meanwhile, halve chicken fillets horizontally. Cook chicken on heated oiled grill plate (or grill or barbecue), until browned and cooked through.
4 Divide potato among plates; top with spinach, chicken then green olive butter.
green olive butter Combine ingredients in small bowl.

prep & cook time 35 minutes serves 4
nutritional count per serving 32.7g total fat
(17g saturated fat); 2345kJ (561 cal);
18.7g carbohydrate; 46.5g protein; 3.5g fibre

cajun chicken with tomato salsa

4 chicken breast fillets (800g), sliced thinly
¼ cup (18g) cajun seasoning
2 teaspoons finely grated lime rind
2 trimmed corn cobs (500g)
2 tablespoons olive oil
1 small red onion (100g), cut into thin wedges
tomato salsa
2 small egg (plum) tomatoes (120g), chopped finely
2 green onions (scallions), sliced thinly
2 teaspoons lime juice
2 teaspoons balsamic vinegar

1 Combine chicken, seasoning and rind in large bowl; mix well. Cut kernels from corn.
2 Make tomato salsa.
3 Heat half the oil in wok; stir-fry chicken mixture, in batches, until cooked through. Remove from wok.
4 Heat remaining oil in wok; stir-fry corn and onion until onion is soft.
5 Return chicken to wok; stir-fry until hot.
6 Serve chicken mixture topped with tomato salsa.
tomato salsa Combine ingredients in small bowl.

prep & cook time 35 minutes **serves** 4
nutritional count per serving 21.3g total fat (4.8g saturated fat); 1919kJ (459 cal); 17g carbohydrate; 47.3g protein; 4.8g fibre

lime chicken on lemon grass skewers

6 x 30cm long (12 inch) fresh lemon grass stalks
⅓ cup (80ml) peanut oil
1 tablespoon finely grated lime rind
¼ cup finely chopped fresh coriander (cilantro)
6 chicken breast fillets (1kg)
¼ cup (60ml) lime juice
2 fresh small red thai (serrano) chillies, chopped finely
⅓ cup (80ml) macadamia oil
1 tablespoon raw sugar
1 clove garlic, crushed

1   Cut 3cm (1 inch) off the end of each lemon grass stalk; reserve stalks. Chop the 3cm pieces finely; combine in large shallow dish with peanut oil, rind and coriander.
2   Cut each chicken fillet into three strips crossways; thread three strips onto each lemon grass stalk 'skewer'. Place skewers in dish with lemon grass marinade; turn skewers to coat chicken in marinade. Cover; refrigerate 3 hours or overnight.
3   Cook skewers on heated oiled barbecue (or grill or grill pan) until chicken is browned and cooked through.
4   Meanwhile, combine remaining ingredients in screw-top jar; shake well. Serve with chicken skewers.

prep & cook time 35 minutes (+ refrigeration) serves 6
nutritional count per serving 33.6g total fat
(6.8g saturated fat); 1906kJ (456 cal);
3g carbohydrate; 35.8g protein; 0.2g fibre

spicy drumsticks with tomato, rocket & herb salad

20 chicken drumsticks (1.5kg)
¼ cup (25g) sumac
¼ cup (60ml) olive oil
½ lebanese cucumber (130g), halved lengthways, sliced thickly
2 medium tomatoes (300g), chopped coarsely
1 medium green capsicum (bell pepper) (200g), chopped finely
¾ cup coarsely chopped fresh flat-leaf parsley
¼ cup coarsely chopped fresh mint
50g (1¾ ounces) baby rocket leaves (arugula)
2 tablespoons lemon juice

1 Combine chicken and sumac in large bowl.
2 Heat 2 tablespoons of the oil in large frying pan; cook chicken, in batches, covered, turning occasionally, until browned and cooked through.
3 Meanwhile, place remaining oil in large bowl with cucumber, tomato, capsicum, herbs, rocket and juice; toss gently.
4 Serve chicken with salad.

prep & cook time 30 minutes serves 4
nutritional count per serving 36.4g total fat (8.7g saturated fat); 2073kJ (496 cal); 3.3g carbohydrate; 38g protein; 2.4g fibre
note Sumac is a purple-red, astringent spice ground from berries growing on shrubs that flourish wild around the Mediterranean; it adds a tart, lemony flavour to dishes. It can be found in Middle-Eastern food stores and most major supermarkets.

chicken parmigiana-style

2 chicken breast fillets (400g)
2 tablespoons plain (all-purpose) flour
1 egg
1 tablespoon milk
1 cup (70g) stale breadcrumbs
¼ cup (60ml) vegetable oil
⅓ cup (85g) bottled tomato pasta sauce, warmed
4 slices ham (185g)
100g (3½ ounces) gruyère cheese, grated coarsely

1 Split chicken fillets in half horizontally. Toss chicken in flour; shake away excess. Dip chicken pieces, one at a time, in combined egg and milk, then in breadcrumbs.
2 Heat oil in large frying pan; shallow-fry chicken, in batches, until browned and cooked through. Drain on absorbent paper.
3 Meanwhile, preheat grill (broiler).
4 Place chicken on oven tray; divide pasta sauce, then ham and finally cheese over chicken. Place under grill until cheese melts.

prep & cook time 30 minutes **serves** 4
nutritional count per serving 31.2g total fat
(9.7g saturated fat); 2178kJ (521 cal);
18.3g carbohydrate; 41.4g protein; 1.3g fibre
note This dish goes well with a parmesan and baby rocket salad.

smoked chicken salad with wild rice

2 cups (400g) wild rice
200g (6½ ounces) seedless red grapes
3 stalks celery (450g), trimmed, sliced thinly
½ cup (60g) roasted pecans
350g (11 ounces) watercress, trimmed
500g (1 pound) smoked chicken breasts, sliced thinly
lime and black pepper dressing
½ cup (125ml) lime juice
½ cup (125ml) olive oil
1 tablespoon caster (superfine) sugar
¼ teaspoon cracked black pepper

1   Cook rice in large saucepan of boiling water, uncovered, until just tender; drain. Rinse under cold water; drain.
2   Meanwhile, make lime and black pepper dressing.
3   Place rice in large bowl with grapes, celery, nuts and half the dressing; toss gently.
4   Divide watercress among serving plates; top with rice salad then chicken. Drizzle with remaining dressing.
lime and black pepper dressing Combine ingredients in screw-top jar; shake well.

prep & cook time 25 minutes serves 6
nutritional count per serving 33.1g total fat
(4.9g saturated fat); 2830kJ (677 cal);
56.4g carbohydrate; 33.7g protein; 9.3g fibre

meat

tamarind-glazed lamb rack with buk choy & orange salad

¼ cup (60ml) tamarind concentrate
¼ cup (60ml) orange juice
2 teaspoons sesame oil
1 tablespoon light brown sugar
4 x 4 french-trimmed lamb cutlet racks (600g)
2 large oranges (600g)
100g (3½ ounces) baby buk choy, leaves separated
100g (3½ ounces) shiitake mushrooms, sliced thickly

1 Preheat oven to 180°C/350°F.
2 Combine tamarind, juice, oil and sugar in small saucepan; reserve 2 tablespoons of the tamarind mixture in large bowl. Bring remaining mixture in pan to the boil. Reduce heat; simmer, uncovered, about 2 minutes or until mixture thickens slightly.
3 Place lamb on metal rack inside large shallow baking pan; brush hot glaze over racks. Cook, uncovered, in oven, about 20 minutes or until racks are cooked as desired. Cover racks; stand 10 minutes.
4 Segment oranges over reserved tamarind mixture in bowl. Add buk choy and mushrooms; toss gently.
5 Cut each lamb rack in half; place two halves on each serving plate, serve with salad.

prep & cook time 35 minutes serves 4
nutritional count per serving 19.1g total fat
(7.8g saturated fat); 1308kJ (313 cal);
16.8g carbohydrate; 17.3g protein; 3.2g fibre

tandoori lamb cutlets

12 lamb cutlets (900g)
½ cup (150g) tandoori paste
¾ cup (200g) plain yogurt
chutney
1 tablespoon vegetable oil
1 small red onion (100g), chopped finely
2 large tomatoes (500g), chopped finely
1 tablespoon lime juice
1 tablespoon sweet chilli sauce
2 tablespoons finely chopped fresh coriander
   (cilantro)
raita
½ lebanese cucumber (130g), chopped finely
2 tablespoons finely chopped fresh mint
¾ cup (200g) plain yogurt

1 Combine lamb with tandoori paste and yogurt in
large bowl.
2 Make chutney; make raita.
3 Cook lamb on heated barbecue (or grill or grill pan)
until browned and cooked through.
4 Serve lamb with separate bowls of chutney and raita.
Top with thinly sliced green onion (scallion), if desired.
chutney Combine ingredients in small bowl.
raita Combine ingredients in small bowl.

prep & cook time 30 minutes serves 4
nutritional count per serving 34g total fat
(11.4g saturated fat); 2199kJ (526 cal);
16.9g carbohydrate; 34.6g protein; 6.2g fibre
note Lamb can be marinated overnight, if you like;
keep, covered, in the refrigerator.

lamb kofta with chilli tomato & yogurt sauce

1kg minced (ground) lamb
1 large brown onion (200g), chopped finely
1 clove garlic, crushed
1 tablespoon ground cumin
2 teaspoons ground turmeric
2 teaspoons ground allspice
1 tablespoon finely chopped fresh mint
2 tablespoons finely chopped fresh flat-leaf parsley
1 egg, beaten lightly
6 pocket pitta breads, quartered
yogurt sauce
¾ cup (200g) low-fat plain yogurt
1 clove garlic, crushed
1 tablespoon finely chopped fresh flat-leaf parsley
chilli tomato sauce
¼ cup (60ml) tomato sauce (ketchup)
¼ cup (60ml) chilli sauce

1   Make yogurt; make chilli tomato sauce.
2   Combine lamb, onion, garlic, spices, herbs and egg in large bowl. Divide mixture into 18 pieces; mould around skewers to form sausage shapes. Cook, in batches, on heated oiled grill plate (or grill or barbecue) until browned and cooked through.
3   Serve kofta with pitta, yogurt sauce and chilli tomato sauce. Accompany with tabbouleh, if you like.
yogurt sauce Combine ingredients in small bowl.
chilli tomato sauce Combine sauces in small bowl.

prep & cook time 30 minutes **serves** 6
nutritional count per serving 14.1g total fat (5.7g saturated fat); 1931kJ (462 cal); 38.2g carbohydrate; 43.2g protein; 3.1g fibre
note Soak 18 bamboo skewers in water for at least 30 minutes to prevent scorching during cooking, or cover the ends with foil.

lamb, spinach & spiced peach salad

20g (¾ ounce) butter
1 teaspoon ground coriander
½ teaspoon ground cardamom
¼ teaspoon ground cinnamon
3 medium peaches (450g), peeled, sliced thickly
2 tablespoons light brown sugar
1 tablespoon raspberry vinegar
800g (1¾ pounds) lamb fillet
1 large red onion (300g), sliced thinly
150g (5 ounces) snow peas, trimmed, sliced thinly
150g (5 ounces) baby spinach leaves
2 fresh long red chillies, sliced thinly
raspberry dressing
120g (4 ounces) raspberries
2 tablespoons raspberry vinegar
2 tablespoons olive oil
1 teaspoon white sugar
1 teaspoon dijon mustard

1   Melt butter in large frying pan; cook spices, stirring, until fragrant. Add peach; cook, stirring, about 2 minutes or until just tender. Add sugar and vinegar; cook, stirring, until sugar dissolves. Remove peach from pan with slotted spoon; place in large bowl.
2   Add lamb to sugar mixture in pan; cook, uncovered, over low heat until lamb is browned both sides and cooked as desired. Cover lamb; stand 10 minutes then slice thickly.
3   Meanwhile, make raspberry dressing.
4   Combine lamb and remaining ingredients in bowl with peach; toss gently. Drizzle dressing over salad.
raspberry dressing Blend or process ingredients until smooth.

prep & cook time 35 minutes serves 4
nutritional count per serving 30.1g total fat
(10g saturated fat); 2337kJ (559 cal);
21.8g carbohydrate; 47g protein; 6g fibre

paprika lamb chops with greek salad

8 lamb loin chops (800g)
2 teaspoons sweet paprika
¼ cup (60ml) olive oil
1 medium red capsicum (bell pepper) (200g),
    chopped coarsely
1 medium green capsicum (bell pepper) (200g),
    chopped coarsely
2 medium tomatoes (300g), chopped coarsely
200g (6½ ounces) fetta cheese, diced into 2cm pieces
1 tablespoon lemon juice
¼ cup firmly packed fresh flat-leaf parsley leaves
1 medium lemon (140g), cut into wedges

1   Sprinkle lamb with paprika. Heat 1 tablespoon of
the oil in large frying pan; cook lamb until browned
and cooked as desired. Cover lamb; stand 5 minutes.
2   Meanwhile, combine capsicum, tomato, cheese, juice,
parsley and remaining oil in large bowl; toss gently.
3   Divide salad and lamb among serving plates; serve
with lemon wedges.

prep & cook time 25 minutes **serves** 4
nutritional count per serving 38.6g total fat
(15.9g saturated fat); 2274kJ (544 cal);
4.7g carbohydrate; 43g protein; 2.4g fibre

grilled lamb with fattoush

1 clove garlic, crushed
1 teaspoon sweet paprika
1 tablespoon sumac
1 teaspoon finely chopped fresh oregano
1 tablespoon water
1 tablespoon olive oil
800g (1¾ pound) lamb fillet
fattoush
1 large pitta bread (80g), split in half
1 lebanese cucumber (130g), chopped coarsely
3 medium tomatoes (450g), seeded, chopped coarsely
5 trimmed red radishes (75g), sliced thinly
3 green onions (scallions), sliced thickly
1 cup coarsely chopped fresh flat-leaf parsley
1 cup coarsely chopped fresh mint
1 baby cos lettuce, torn
2 tablespoons sumac
⅓ cup (80ml) lemon juice
¼ cup (60ml) olive oil

1   Combine garlic, paprika, sumac, oregano, the water, oil and lamb in medium bowl; turn to coat lamb.
2   Cook lamb on grill pan (or grill or barbecue) until browned and cooked as desired. Cover lamb; stand 10 minutes then slice thickly.
3   Meanwhile, make fattoush. Serve lamb with fattoush.
fattoush   Toast pitta under preheated grill. Combine cucumber, tomato, radish, onion, herbs and lettuce in large bowl. Place sumac, juice and oil in screw-top jar; shake well. Pour dressing over salad; toss gently. Break pitta into small pieces over salad just before serving.

prep & cook time 35 minutes serves 4
nutritional count per serving 32.7g total fat
(9.1g saturated fat); 2274kJ (544 cal);
14.3g carbohydrate; 45.7g protein; 4.4g fibre

lamb schnitzel with caper herb mash & anchovy mayonnaise

4 lamb steaks (600g)
¼ cup (35g) plain (all-purpose) flour
2 eggs, beaten lightly
1 tablespoon milk
2 cups (140g) stale breadcrumbs
½ cup (40g) finely grated parmesan cheese
vegetable oil, for shallow-frying

caper herb mash
1kg (2 pounds) potatoes, chopped coarsely
½ cup (125ml) pouring cream, warmed
50g (1¾ ounces) butter, melted
2 tablespoons rinsed, drained baby capers,
2 tablespoons finely chopped fresh chives
¼ cup coarsely chopped fresh flat-leaf parsley

anchovy mayonnaise
½ cup (150g) whole-egg mayonnaise
4 drained anchovy fillets, chopped finely
1 tablespoon lemon juice
1 tablespoon warm water

1 Using meat mallet, pound each steak between sheets of plastic wrap until 5mm (¼ inch) thick. Place flour in medium shallow bowl; whisk egg and milk in separate medium shallow bowl. Combine breadcrumbs and cheese in a third medium shallow bowl. Coat steaks, one at a time, in flour, then egg mixture, then breadcrumb mixture. Place schnitzels, in single layer, on tray. Cover; refrigerate.
2 Make caper herb mash; make anchovy mayonnaise.
3 Heat oil in large frying pan; shallow-fry schnitzels, in batches, until browned and cooked as desired. Drain on absorbent paper; cover to keep warm.
4 Divide caper herb mash and schnitzels among serving plates; drizzle with anchovy mayonnaise.
caper herb mash Boil, steam or microwave potato until tender; drain. Mash potato in large bowl with cream and butter; cover to keep warm. Stir in capers and herbs just before serving.
anchovy mayonnaise Whisk ingredients in small bowl until combined.

prep & cook time 35 minutes serves 4
nutritional count per serving 69.8g total fat
(26.6g saturated fat); 4682kJ (1120 cal);
67.9g carbohydrate; 52.7g protein; 5.8g fibre

veal steaks with italian white bean salad

1 tablespoon olive oil
8 veal steaks (680g)
½ cup (125ml) beef stock
60g (2 ounces) butter
italian white bean salad
100g (3½ ounces) baby rocket leaves (arugula)
1 large tomato (250g), chopped coarsely
½ cup firmly packed basil leaves, torn
800g (30 ounces) canned white beans, rinsed, drained
1 tablespoon finely chopped fresh chives
¼ cup (60ml) lemon juice
2 cloves garlic, crushed
¼ cup (60ml) olive oil

1 Make italian white bean salad.
2 Heat oil in large frying pan; cook veal, in batches, until browned and cooked as desired. Remove from pan; cover to keep warm.
3 Pour stock into same pan; bring to the boil, stirring. Add butter, stir until butter melts. Reduce heat; simmer, stirring, 2 minutes. Serve veal, drizzled with sauce, with italian white bean salad.
italian white bean salad Combine rocket, tomato, basil and beans in large bowl. Combine chives, juice, garlic and oil in screw-top jar; shake well. Pour dressing over salad; toss gently to combine.

prep & cook time 25 minutes **serves** 4
nutritional count per serving 35.2g total fat (11.9g saturated fat); 2399kJ (574 cal); 16g carbohydrate; 45.7g protein; 7.8g fibre
note Any variety of canned white beans are suitable, including cannellini, butter and haricot.

mustard veal with polenta & spinach purée

⅓ cup (95g) wholegrain mustard
2 tablespoons coarsely chopped fresh oregano
2 cloves garlic, crushed
4 veal chops (600g)
4 large egg (plum) tomatoes (360g), halved
2 cups (500ml) water
1 teaspoon salt
1 cup (170g) polenta
¾ cup (180ml) skimmed milk
¼ cup (20g) finely grated parmesan cheese
2kg (4 pounds) spinach, trimmed
2 cloves garlic, crushed, extra
2 drained anchovy fillets
2 tablespoons lemon juice
¼ cup (60ml) beef stock

1   Combine mustard, oregano and garlic in small bowl; brush both sides of veal with mustard mixture.
2   Cook veal and tomato, in batches, on heated oiled grill pan (or grill or barbecue) until veal is browned and cooked as desired and tomato is tender.
3   Meanwhile, bring combined water and salt to the boil in medium saucepan. Stir in polenta; cook, stirring, about 10 minutes or until polenta thickens. Stir in milk; cook, stirring, about 5 minutes or until polenta thickens. Stir in cheese.
4   Boil, steam or microwave spinach until just wilted; squeeze out excess liquid. Blend or process spinach with remaining ingredients until puréed.
5   Serve veal with tomato, polenta and spinach purée.

prep & cook time 35 minutes serves 4
nutritional count per serving 7.3g total fat
(2.4g saturated fat); 1643kJ (393 cal);
37.1g carbohydrate; 38.1g protein; 11g fibre

hamburger with a twist

80g (2¾ ounces) gorgonzola cheese, crumbled
¼ cup (60g) sour cream
400g (13 ounces) minced (ground) beef
120g (4 ounce) sausage mince
1 small brown onion (80g), chopped finely
1 tablespoon barbecue sauce
2 teaspoons worcestershire sauce
½ cup (75g) drained sun-dried tomatoes in oil,
    chopped finely
4 hamburger buns (360g)
50g (1¾ ounces) baby rocket leaves (arugula)
170g (5½ ounces) marinated artichoke hearts,
    drained, quartered

1   Blend or process half the cheese with the sour cream
until smooth. Stir in remaining cheese.
2   Combine both minces, onion, sauces and tomato in
medium bowl; shape mixture into four patties.
3   Cook patties in heated oiled large frying pan until
browned and cooked through.
4   Preheat grill (broiler). Halve buns; toast, cut-side up,
under grill. Sandwich rocket, patties, gorgonzola cream
and artichoke between bun halves.

prep & cook time 25 minutes serves 4
nutritional count per serving 32.5g total fat
(15.7g saturated fat), 2525kJ (604 cal);
40.6g carbohydrate; 34.6g protein; 6.1g fibre

stir-fried mexican beef

750g (1½ pounds) beef eye fillet, sliced thinly
35g (1 ounce) packet taco seasoning
1 tablespoon peanut oil
1 large red onion (300g), sliced thinly
1 medium red capsicum (bell pepper) (200g),
    sliced thinly
1 medium yellow capsicum (bell pepper) (200g),
    sliced thinly
4 small tomatoes (520g), seeded, sliced thinly
2 tablespoons fresh coriander (cilantro) leaves

1   Combine beef and seasoning in medium bowl. Heat
half the oil in wok; stir-fry beef mixture and onion, in
batches, until well browned. Remove from wok.
2   Heat remaining oil in wok, stir-fry capsicum until
just tender.
3   Return beef mixture to wok with tomato and
coriander; stir-fry until hot.

prep & cook time 30 minutes serves 4
nutritional count per serving 14.1g total fat
(4.9g saturated fat); 1455kJ (349 cal);
10.8g carbohydrate; 42.5g protein; 3.2g fibre
note You can also use beef rib eye, rump, sirloin or
topside in this recipe.

chilli beef stir-fry

4 fresh long red chillies, sliced thinly
2.5cm (1 inch) piece fresh ginger (15g),
    chopped coarsely
1 small red onion (100g), chopped coarsely
⅓ cup (75g) firmly packed light brown sugar
1 tablespoon fish sauce
2 tablespoons vegetable oil
650g (1¼ pounds) beef strips
6 green onions (scallions), cut into 5cm (2 inch) lengths
½ medium wombok (napa cabbage) (500g),
    chopped coarsely
1 tablespoon fish sauce, extra
¼ cup firmly packed thai basil leaves

1 Blend or process chilli, ginger, red onion, sugar, sauce
and oil until mixture forms a coarse paste. Stir-fry chilli
mixture in heated oiled wok until fragrant. Add beef;
stir-fry until browned.
2 Add green onion and wombok to wok; stir-fry until
cabbage wilts. Add extra sauce and basil; stir-fry until
hot. Serve with steamed rice, if you like.

prep & cook time 30 minutes serves 4
nutritional count per serving 17g total fat
(4.4g saturated fat); 1731kJ (414 cal);
24.4g carbohydrate; 39g protein; 5.9g fibre

steaks with parsnip mash

4 beef sirloin steaks (880g)
½ cup (125ml) plum sauce
⅓ cup (80ml) tomato sauce (ketchup)
⅓ cup (80ml) worcestershire sauce
2 cloves garlic, crushed
2 green onions (scallions), chopped finely
1kg (2 pounds) potatoes, chopped coarsely
2 medium parsnips (500g), chopped coarsely
40g (1¼ ounces) butter, chopped
⅓ cup (80ml) cream
250g (8 ounces) baby spinach leaves

1 Combine beef in large bowl with sauces, garlic and
onion; toss to coat beef in marinade. Cover; refrigerate
30 minutes.
2 Meanwhile, boil, steam or microwave potato and
parsnip until just tender; drain. Mash with butter and
cream in large bowl until smooth. Cover to keep warm.
3 Drain beef; discard marinade. Cook beef in heated
oiled grill pan (or grill or barbecue) until browned and
cooked as you like.
4 Boil, steam or microwave spinach until just wilted;
drain. Serve beef with mash and spinach.

prep & cook time 30 minutes (+ refrigeration) serves 4
nutritional count per serving 31.6g total fat
(17.1g saturated fat); 3382kJ (809 cal);
72.7g carbohydrate; 54.7g protein; 9g fibre

thai char-grilled beef salad

600g (1¼ pound) piece beef rump steak
2 teaspoons sesame oil
⅓ cup (80ml) kecap manis
1 cup loosely packed fresh mint leaves
1 cup loosely packed fresh coriander (cilantro) leaves
½ cup loosely packed fresh thai basil leaves
6 green onions (scallions), sliced thinly
5 shallots (60g), sliced thinly
250g (8 ounces) cherry tomatoes, halved
1 lebanese cucumber (130g), seeded, sliced thinly
10 kaffir lime leaves, shredded finely
100g (3½ ounces) mixed salad leaves
sweet and sour dressing
½ cup (125ml) lime juice
¼ cup (60ml) fish sauce
2 teaspoons white sugar
2 fresh small red thai (serrano) chillies, sliced thinly

1 Place beef in shallow dish; brush all over with combined oil and kecap manis. Cover; refrigerate 30 minutes.
2 Meanwhile, combine herbs, onion, shallot, tomato and cucumber in large bowl; toss gently.
3 Make sweet and sour dressing.
4 Cook beef on heated oiled grill plate (or grill or barbecue) until charred lightly and cooked as desired. Cover beef; stand 10 minutes then slice thinly.
5 Place beef, lime leaves and salad leaves in bowl with herb mixture. Add sweet and sour dressing; toss gently.
sweet and sour dressing Combine ingredients in screw-top jar; shake well.

prep & cook time 25 minutes (+ refrigeration) serves 4
nutritional count per serving 9.6g total fat (3.3g saturated fat); 1154kJ (276 cal); 7.4g carbohydrate; 36.6g protein; 3.3g fibre
notes Thai basil, also known as horapa, has a sweet licorice flavour; it is available from Asian grocery stores and most major supermarkets.
Rib-eye, boneless sirloin or eye fillet steaks are all good substitutes for rump in this recipe.

teriyaki steak

750g (1½ pound) piece beef rump steak, sliced thinly
¼ cup (60ml) rice vinegar
¼ cup (60ml) kecap manis
1 tablespoon light brown sugar
¼ cup (60ml) lime juice
1 clove garlic, crushed
2 fresh small red thai (serrano) chillies, chopped finely
1 teaspoon sesame oil
1 tablespoon peanut oil
1 large carrot (180g), cut into matchsticks
200g (6½ ounces) white cabbage, shredded finely
¼ cup (50g) japanese pickled cucumber

1   Combine beef, vinegar, kecap manis, sugar, juice, garlic, chilli and sesame oil in large bowl, cover; refrigerate 3 hours or overnight. Drain beef; reserve marinade.
2   Heat peanut oil in wok; stir-fry beef, in batches, until browned all over. Cover beef to keep warm.
3   Pour reserved marinade into wok; bring to the boil. Boil, uncovered, until sauce reduces by a third.
4   Divide combined carrot and cabbage among serving plates; top with beef, drizzle with sauce. Serve with pickled cucumber and, if you like, steamed rice.

prep & cook time 20 minutes (+ refrigeration) **serves** 4
nutritional count per serving 14.5g total fat
(4.7g saturated fat); 1413kJ (338 cal);
6.6g carbohydrate; 42.7g protein; 2.2g fibre
note Japanese pickled cucumber has a sour taste and is available, packaged in brine, from most Asian food stores.

beef salad with blue-cheese dressing

500g (1 pound) baby new potatoes, quartered
1 tablespoon olive oil
4 beef fillet steaks (500g)
300g (10 ounces) green beans, trimmed,
   halved crossways
200g (6½ ounces) cherry tomatoes, halved
100g (3¼ ounces) baby rocket leaves (arugula)
blue-cheese dressing
¼ cup (60ml) olive oil
2 cloves garlic, crushed
¼ cup (60ml) orange juice
60g (2 ounces) blue cheese, crumbled

1 Preheat oven to 220°C/425°F.
2 Place potato, in single layer, in large shallow baking
tin; drizzle with oil. Roast, uncovered, about 20 minutes
or until browned lightly and tender.
3 Meanwhile, make blue-cheese dressing.
4 Cook beef on heated oiled grill plate (or grill or
barbecue) until browned both sides and cooked as
desired. Cover; stand 5 minutes then slice thinly.
5 Meanwhile, boil, steam or microwave beans until
just tender; drain.
6 Combine beef, beans and potato in large bowl with
tomato and rocket, drizzle with dressing; toss gently.
blue-cheese dressing Combine ingredients in
screw-top jar; shake well.

prep & cook time 25 minutes serves 4
nutritional count per serving 26.2g total fat
(7.8g saturated fat); 1981kJ (474 cal);
21.3g carbohydrate; 34.9g protein; 6g fibre

gingered pork with vegetables

700g (1½ pounds) pork fillets, sliced thinly
¼ cup finely chopped fresh coriander (cilantro)
4cm (1½ inch) piece fresh ginger (20g), grated
2 tablespoons rice vinegar
2 tablespoons peanut oil
125g (4 ounces) baby corn, halved lengthways
1 medium red capsicum (bell pepper) (200g),
    sliced thinly
100g (3¼ ounces) snow peas, halved
2 tablespoons light soy sauce
250g (8 ounces) spinach, trimmed
3 cups (240g) bean sprouts
½ cup fresh coriander (cilantro) leaves, extra

1 Place pork in medium bowl with coriander, ginger and vinegar; mix to combine. Cover; refrigerate 3 hours or overnight.
2 Heat half the oil in wok; stir-fry pork mixture, in batches, until pork is browned and cooked through. Remove from wok.
3 Heat remaining oil in wok. Stir-fry corn, capsicum and snow peas until just tender; remove from wok. Return pork to wok with soy sauce; stir-fry until heated through. Just before serving, return cooked vegetables to wok and toss gently with pork, spinach, sprouts and extra coriander until spinach just wilts.

prep & cook time 25 minutes (+ refrigeration) serves 4
nutritional count per serving 13.8g total fat
(3.3g saturated fat); 1471kJ (352 cal);
9.4g carbohydrate; 44.5g protein; 5.2g fibre

chilli pork with oyster sauce

1 tablespoon peanut oil
450g (14 ounces) pork fillets, sliced thinly
1 clove garlic, crushed
1 medium white onion (150g), sliced thinly
1 large red capsicum (bell pepper) (350g),
    sliced thinly
1 small green zucchini (90g), sliced thinly
1 small yellow zucchini (90g), sliced thinly
¼ cup (60ml) oyster sauce
1 tablespoon sweet chilli sauce
1 tablespoon coarsely chopped fresh coriander
    (cilantro)

1   Heat oil in wok; stir-fry pork, in batches, until browned.
Remove from wok.
2   Add garlic and onion to wok; stir-fry until onion is
just softened. Add capsicum and zucchini to wok; stir-fry
until vegetables are just softened.
3   Return pork to wok, add sauces; stir-fry until hot.
Serve stir-fry sprinkled with coriander.

prep & cook time 25 minutes serves 4
nutritional count per serving 7.8g total fat
(1.9g saturated fat); 957kJ (229 cal);
10.6g carbohydrate; 27.6g protein; 2.4g fibre

spicy pork ribs

1.5kg (3 pounds) trimmed pork spare rib slabs
¾ cup (180ml) light soy sauce
1 egg, beaten lightly
¼ cup (35g) plain (all-purpose) flour
2 tablespoons vegetable oil
½ cup (125ml) rice wine
½ cup (100g) firmly packed light brown sugar
¼ cup (50g) yellow mustard seeds
⅓ cup finely chopped fresh coriander (cilantro)
3 cloves garlic, crushed
4cm (1½ inch) piece fresh ginger (20g), grated
3 teaspoons dried chilli flakes
1 teaspoon five-spice powder
½ teaspoon cayenne pepper

1 Cut pork into individual rib pieces. Place ribs in large saucepan, cover with water; bring to the boil. Simmer, uncovered, about 10 minutes or until ribs are almost cooked through. Drain; pat dry with absorbent paper.
2 Blend ¼ cup of the soy sauce with the egg and flour in large bowl. Add ribs; toss to coat in soy mixture.
3 Heat oil in wok; stir-fry ribs, in batches, until browned all over. Remove from wok.
4 Add remaining soy sauce and remaining ingredients to wok; stir-fry until sugar dissolves. Return ribs to wok; stir-fry until heated through.

prep & cook time 30 minutes serves 4
nutritional count per serving 23.5g total fat
(6.5g saturated fat); 2441kJ (584 cal);
32.4g carbohydrate; 56.3g protein; 0.7g fibre
notes Ask your butcher to cut the pork ribs 'american-style' so that as much fat as possible has been removed, leaving only the tender, flavoursome meat.
Serve with steamed rice and individual finger bowls filled with water and a few slices of lemon, if desired.

pork fillet with apple and leek

800g (1¾ pounds) pork fillets
¾ cup (180ml) chicken stock
2 medium leeks (700g), sliced thickly
1 clove garlic, crushed
2 tablespoons light brown sugar
2 tablespoons red wine vinegar
2 medium apples (300g)
10g (½ ounce) butter
1 tablespoon light brown sugar, extra
400g (13 ounces) baby carrots, trimmed, halved
250g (8 ounces) asparagus, trimmed,
    chopped coarsely
8 medium yellow patty-pan squash (100g), quartered

1 Preheat oven to 220°C/425°F.
2 Place pork in large baking pan; bake, uncovered, about 25 minutes or until pork is browned and cooked through. Cover; stand 5 minutes then slice thickly.
3 Meanwhile, heat half the stock in medium frying pan; cook leek and garlic, stirring, until leek softens and browns slightly. Add sugar and vinegar; cook, stirring, about 5 minutes or until leek caramelises. Add remaining stock; bring to the boil. Reduce heat; simmer, uncovered, about 5 minutes or until liquid reduces by half. Place leek mixture in medium bowl; cover to keep warm.
4 Peel, core and halve apples; cut into thick slices. Melt butter in frying pan; cook apple and extra sugar, stirring, until apple is browned and tender.
5 Boil, steam or microwave carrot, asparagus and squash separately, until just tender; drain. Serve vegetables topped with pork, caramelised apple and leek.

prep & cook time 35 minutes serves 4
nutritional count per serving 8.8g total fat (3.6g saturated fat); 1822kJ (436 cal); 26.6g carbohydrate; 58.2g protein; 8.8g fibre

glossary

ALLSPICE also known as pimento or jamaican pepper; available whole or ground. Tastes like a blend of cinnamon, clove and nutmeg – all spices.

ARTICHOKE HEARTS tender centre of the globe artichoke; purchased, in brine, canned or in glass jars.

BAMBOO SHOOTS the tender shoots of bamboo plants, available in cans; must be rinsed and drained before use.

BASIL an aromatic herb; there are many types, but the most commonly used is sweet, or common, basil.
thai also known as horapa; has smallish leaves and a sweet licorice/aniseed taste. Available from Asian food stores, some supermarkets and greengrocers.
purple also known as opal basil; has large purple leaves and a sweet, almost gingery flavour. It has better keeping properties than most other basils. If unavailable, use common basil.

BEANS
borlotti also known as roman beans or pink beans. Interchangeable with pinto beans as they are both pale pink or beige with dark red streaks.
cannellini small white bean similar in appearance and flavour to other white beans (great northern, navy or haricot), all of which can be substituted for the other. Available dried or canned.
kidney medium-sized red bean, slightly floury in texture yet sweet in flavour.
sprouts also known as bean shoots; tender new growths of assorted beans and seeds germinated for consumption.
white see cannellini beans.

BREADCRUMBS
packaged fine-textured, crunchy, purchased white breadcrumbs.
stale one- or two-day-old bread made into crumbs by blending or processing.

BUK CHOY also known as bok choy, pak choi, chinese white cabbage or chinese chard; has a fresh, mild mustard taste. Use both stems and leaves. Baby buk choy, also known as pak kat farang or shanghai bok choy, is smaller and more tender than buk choy.

BUTTER use salted or unsalted (sweet) butter; 125g is equal to one stick of butter (4 ounces).

CAJUN SEASONING a blend of assorted herbs and spices that can include paprika, basil, onion, fennel, thyme, cayenne and tarragon.

CAPERS the grey-green buds of a warm climate shrub (usually Mediterranean); sold either dried and salted or pickled in a vinegar brine. Baby capers are very small and have a fuller-flavour. Capers must be rinsed well before using.

CHEESE
blue mould-treated cheeses mottled with blue veining. Varieties include firm and crumbly stilton types to mild, creamy brie-like cheeses.
cream cheese known as Philadelphia or Philly, a soft, cows-milk cheese; sold at supermarkets. Also available as a spreadable light cream cheese – a blend of cottage and cream cheeses.
goat's made from goat's milk, has an earthy, strong taste; available in both soft and firm textures, in various shapes and sizes, and sometimes rolled in ash or herbs.
gorgonzola a creamy blue cheese having a mild, sweet taste.
gruyere a Swiss cheese having small holes and a nutty, slightly salty flavour.
haloumi a firm, cream-coloured sheep-milk cheese matured in brine; somewhat like a minty, salty fetta in flavour, haloumi can be grilled or fried, briefly, without breaking down. Should be eaten while still warm as it becomes tough and rubbery on cooling.
mascarpone a cultured cream product made in much the same way as yogurt. Is whitish to creamy yellow in colour, with a soft, creamy texture and a rich, sweet, slightly acidic, taste.
pizza a blend of grated mozzarella, cheddar and parmesan cheeses.

CHILLI available in many types and sizes; generally the smaller the chilli, the hotter it is. Use rubber gloves when seeding and chopping fresh chillies as they can burn your skin. Removing seeds and membranes lessens the heat level.
cayenne pepper a long, thin-fleshed, extremely hot red chilli usually sold dried and ground.
flakes, dried deep-red, dehydrated chilli slices and whole seeds.
green any unripened chilli.
long red available both fresh and dried; a generic term used for any moderately hot, long (6cm-8cm), thin chilli.
powder made from ground chillies; it can be used as a substitute for fresh chillies in the proportion of ½ teaspoon ground chilli powder to 1 medium chopped fresh chilli.

red thai a small, hot, red chilli.

CIABATTA in Italian, the word means 'slipper', which is the traditional shape of this popular crisp-crusted white bread.

CORIANDER also known as pak chee, cilantro or chinese parsley; bright-green leafy herb with a pungent flavour. Both the stems and roots of coriander are also used in cooking; wash well before using. Also available ground or as seeds; these should not be substituted for fresh coriander as the tastes are completely different.

COS LETTUCE also known as romaine.

COUSCOUS a fine, grain-like cereal product made from semolina.

CREAM we use fresh cream, also known as pure cream and pouring cream, unless otherwise stated.

CUMIN also known as zeera or comino; has a spicy, nutty flavour.

CURRY
curry powder a blend of ground spices used for convenience when making Indian food. Choose mild or hot to suit your taste and the recipe.
green paste the hottest of the traditional pastes; contains chilli, garlic, onion, salt, lemon grass, spices and galangal.
tandoori paste a highly-seasoned classic East Indian marinade flavoured with garlic, tamarind, ginger, coriander, chilli and other spices and used to give foods the authentic red-orange tint of tandoor oven cooking.
tikka paste a medium-mild paste of chilli, coriander, cumin, lentil flour, garlic, ginger, oil, turmeric, fennel, pepper, cloves, cinnamon and cardamom.

EGGPLANT also known as aubergine.

EVAPORATED MILK unsweetened canned milk from which water has been extracted by evaporation.

FENNEL also known as finocchio or anise; a white to very pale green-white, firm, crisp, roundish vegetable about 8-12cm in diameter. The bulb has a slightly sweet, anise flavour but the leaves have a much stronger taste. Also the name given to dried seeds having a licorice flavour.

FISH FILLETS, FIRM WHITE blue eye, bream, flathead, swordfish, ling, whiting, jewfish, snapper or sea perch are all good choices. Check for any small pieces of bone in the fillets and use tweezers to remove them.

FIVE-SPICE POWDER also known as chinese five-spice; a fragrant mixture of ground cinnamon, cloves, star anise, sichuan pepper and fennel seeds.

FLOUR
plain an all-purpose wheat flour.
self-raising plain flour sifted with baking powder in the proportion of 1 cup flour to 2 teaspoons baking powder.

GINGER also known as green or root ginger; the thick root of a tropical plant.
ground also known as powdered ginger; is used as a flavouring in cakes. Cannot be substituted for fresh ginger.

GNOCCHI Italian 'dumplings' made of potatoes, semolina or flour.

KAFFIR LIME LEAVES also known as bai magrood. Aromatic leaves of a citrus tree; two glossy dark green leaves joined end to end, forming a rounded hourglass shape. A strip of fresh lime peel may be substituted for each kaffir lime leaf.

KECAP MANIS *see sauces, soy.*

KUMARA the Polynesian name of an orange-fleshed sweet potato often confused with yam.

LEBANESE CUCUMBER short, slender and thin-skinned. Probably the most popular variety because of its tender, edible skin, tiny, yielding seeds and sweet, fresh flavoursome taste.

LEMON GRASS a tall, clumping, lemon-smelling and -tasting, sharp-edged grass; the white lower part of the stem is used, finely chopped, in cooking.

LENTILS (red, brown, yellow) dried pulses often identified by and named after their colour; also known as dhal.

MAYONNAISE we use whole-egg mayonnaise in our recipes.

MINCE also known as ground meat.

MUSHROOMS
button small, cultivated white mushrooms with a mild flavour.
chestnut have small brown caps, long, thin white stems and a strong, nutty flavour. They also have a low moisture content, so need slightly longer cooking than some of the other mushrooms. Trim woody ends from stems before use.
enoki clumps of long, spaghetti-like stems with tiny, snowy white caps.
flat large, flat mushrooms with a rich earthy flavour. They are sometimes misnamed field mushrooms, which are wild mushrooms.

oyster also known as abalone; grey-white mushroom shaped like a fan. Prized for their smooth texture and subtle, oyster-like flavour.
shiitake when fresh are also known as chinese black, forest or golden oak mushrooms; although cultivated, they are large and meaty and have the earthiness and taste of wild mushrooms. When dried, they are known as donko or dried chinese mushrooms; rehydrate before use.

MUSTARD SEEDS are available in black, brown or yellow varieties. They are available from major supermarkets and health-food shops.

NOODLES
bean thread vermicelli made from mung bean flour. Fine, delicate noodles also known as wun sen, cellophane or glass noodles (because they are transparent when cooked). Available dried in various-sized bundles. Must be soaked to soften before use.
dried rice stick made from rice flour and water; available flat and wide or very thin (vermicelli). Should be soaked in boiling water to soften.
egg, fresh also known as ba mee or yellow noodles. Made from wheat flour and eggs. Range in size from very fine strands to wide, thick spaghetti-like pieces as thick as a shoelace.
hokkien also known as stir-fry noodles; fresh wheat noodles resembling thick, yellow-brown spaghetti needing no pre-cooking before being used.
ramen, fresh comes in various shapes and lengths. They may be fat, thin or even ribbon-like, as well as straight or wrinkled. While more often sold dried, fresh ramen is available from some Asian food stores. Substitute with reconstituted dried noodles.
soba a thin spaghetti-like pale brown noodle from Japan; made from buckwheat and varying proportions of wheat flour.

ONIONS
green also known as scallion or, incorrectly, shallot; an immature onion picked before the bulb has formed, having a long, bright-green edible stalk.
red also known as spanish, red spanish or bermuda onion; a sweet-flavoured, large, purple-red onion.
shallots also called french shallots, golden shallots or eschalots; small, brown-skinned, elongated members of the onion family.

spring onions with small white bulbs and long, narrow, green-leafed tops.

PAPRIKA ground, dried, sweet red capsicum (bell pepper); there are many types available, including sweet, hot, mild and smoked.

PARSLEY, FLAT-LEAF also known as continental or italian parsley.

PASTA
orecchiette small disc-shaped pasta; translates literally as 'little ears'.
pappardelle a wide, ribbon-like pasta with scalloped sides; is sometimes sold as lasagnette or even lasagne. Any wide, long pasta can be used.
rigatoni a form of tube-shaped pasta. It is larger than penne and is usually ridged, The end doesn't terminate at an angle, like penne's does.
risoni small rice-shaped pasta.
tagliatelle flat strips of pasta, slightly narrower and thinner than fettuccine.

PATTY-PAN SQUASH also known as crookneck or custard marrow pumpkins; a round, slightly flat summer squash being yellow to pale-green in colour and having a scalloped edge. It has a firm white flesh and a distinct flavour.

PITTA also known as lebanese bread; a wheat-flour pocket bread sold in large, flat pieces that separate into two thin rounds. Also available in small thick pieces called pocket pitta.

PIZZA BASES pre-packaged for home-made pizzas. They come in a variety of sizes (snack or family) and thicknesses (thin and crispy or thick).

POLENTA also known as cornmeal; a flour-like cereal made of ground corn (maize). Also the name of the dish made from it.

PRAWN also known as shrimp.

PROSCIUTTO a kind of unsmoked Italian ham; salted, air-cured and aged, it is usually eaten uncooked.

RICE
arborio small, round-grained rice, suited to absorb a large amount of liquid.
jasmine fragrant long-grained rice; white rice can be substituted, but will not taste the same.
wild rice blend a packaged mixture of white long-grain and dark brown wild rice. The latter is the seed of a North American aquatic grass, which has a distinctively nutty flavour and a crunchy, resilient texture.

115

ROCKET also known as arugula, rugula and rucola; a peppery-tasting green leaf. Baby rocket leaves are both smaller and less peppery.

SAKE Japan's favourite wine, made from fermented rice. If sake is unavailable, dry sherry, vermouth or brandy can be substituted. Cooking sake (containing salt) is also available.

SAMBAL OELEK (also ulek or olek) Indonesian in origin; a salty paste made from ground chillies and vinegar. Found in supermarkets and Asian food stores.

SAUCES
black bean a Chinese sauce made from fermented soya beans, spices, water and wheat flour.
char siu a Chinese barbecue sauce made from sugar, water, salt, fermented soybean paste, honey, soy sauce, malt syrup and spices. It can be found at most supermarkets.
chilli we use a hot Chinese variety made from red thai chillies, salt and vinegar. Use sparingly, increasing the quantity to suit your taste.
fish also called nam pla or nuoc nam; made from pulverised salted fermented fish, most often anchovies. Has a pungent smell and strong taste, so use sparingly.
hoisin a thick, sweet and spicy Chinese paste made from salted fermented soya beans, onions and garlic.
oyster Asian in origin, this rich, brown sauce is made from oysters and their brine, cooked with salt and soy sauce, and thickened with starches.
plum a thick, sweet and sour dipping sauce made from plums, vinegar, sugar, chillies and spices.
soy made from fermented soya beans. Several variations are available in most supermarkets and Asian food stores. We use japanese soy sauce, unless otherwise indicated. It is the best table soy and the one to choose if you only want one type.
dark soy deep brown, almost black in colour; rich, with a thicker consistency than other types. Pungent but not that salty; it is good for marinating.
japanese soy an all-purpose low-sodium soy sauce made with more wheat content than its Chinese counterparts.
kecap manis also known as ketjap manis; a thick soy sauce with added sugar and spices. Depending on the brand, the soy's sweetness is derived from the addition of either molasses or palm sugar when brewed.

light soy a fairly thin, pale but salty tasting sauce; used in dishes in which the natural colour of the ingredients is to be maintained. Do not confuse with salt-reduced or low-sodium soy sauces.
sweet chilli a mild Thai sauce made from red chillies, sugar, garlic and vinegar.
tomato also known as ketchup or catsup; a flavoured condiment made from tomatoes, vinegar and spices.
tomato pasta made from a blend of tomatoes, herbs and spices.
worcestershire a thin, dark-brown spicy sauce made from garlic, soy sauce, lime, tamarind, onions, molasses, anchovies, vinegar and seasonings.

SILVER BEET also known as swiss chard and blettes; mistakenly called spinach.

SNOW PEAS also called mange tout (eat all). Snow pea tendrils, the growing shoots of the plant, are also available at greengrocers. Snow pea sprouts are the tender new growths of snow peas.

SPINACH also known as english spinach and, incorrectly, silver beet.

STOCK available in cans, bottles or tetra packs. Stock cubes or powder can be used. As a guide, 1 teaspoon of stock powder or 1 small crumbled stock cube mixed with 1 cup (250ml) water will give a fairly strong stock. Be aware of the salt and fat content of stock cubes and powders and prepared stocks.

SUGAR
brown very soft, finely granulated sugar retaining molasses for its characteristic colour and flavour. Dark brown sugar may be substituted.
caster also known as superfine or finely granulated table sugar.
raw natural brown coarse-grain sugar.
white a coarsely granulated table sugar, also known as crystal sugar.

SUGAR SNAP PEAS are also known as honey snap peas; fresh small pea that can be eaten whole, pod and all, similarly to snow peas.

SUMAC a purple-red, astringent spice that is ground from berries growing on shrubs that flourish wild around the Mediterranean; adds a tart, lemony flavour. Available from spice shops and major supermarkets.

TACO SEASONING MIX is meant to duplicate the taste of a Mexican sauce made from oregano, cumin, chillies and other spices.

TAMARIND CONCENTRATE the commercial distillation of tamarind pulp into a condensed paste. Used straight from the container, with no soaking or straining required, although it can be diluted with water according to taste. Found in supermarkets and Asian food stores. It adds a tart, sour taste to food.

TOMATO
paste triple-concentrated tomato puree.
puree canned pureed tomatoes (not tomato paste).
semi-dried partially dried tomato pieces in olive oil; these are softer and juicier than sun-dried, but are not a preserve, so do not keep as long as sun-dried.
sun-dried we use sun-dried tomatoes in oil, unless otherwise specified.

TURMERIC a rhizome related to galangal and ginger; it adds a golden-yellow colour to food. If fresh, it must be grated or pounded to release its somewhat acrid aroma and pungent flavour. It is also available ground.

VINEGAR
balsamic originally from Modena, Italy, there are now many balsamic vinegars on the market ranging in pungency and quality depending on how long they have been aged. Is a deep rich brown colour and has a sweet and sour flavour. Quality can be determined up to a point by price; use the most expensive sparingly.
brown malt made from fermented malt and beech shavings.
raspberry made from fresh raspberries steeped in a white wine vinegar.
red wine based on fermented red wine.
rice a colourless vinegar made from fermented rice, sugar and salt. Also known as seasoned rice vinegar.
sherry made from a blend of wines and left in wood vats to mature where they develop a rich mellow flavour.
white made from spirit of cane sugar.
white wine made from white wine.

WATERCRESS one of the cress family, a large group of peppery greens. Highly perishable, so must be used as soon as possible after purchase.

WOMBOK also known as peking cabbage, chinese cabbage or petsai. Elongated in shape with pale green, crinkly leaves, this is the most common cabbage in South-East Asian cooking.

YOGURT we use plain, unflavoured yogurt unless otherwise specified.

ZUCCHINI also known as courgette.

conversion chart

MEASURES

One Australian metric measuring cup holds approximately 250ml; one Australian metric tablespoon holds 20ml; one Australian metric teaspoon holds 5ml.

The difference between one country's measuring cups and another's is within a two- or three-teaspoon variance, and will not affect your cooking results. North America, New Zealand and the United Kingdom use a 15ml tablespoon.

All cup and spoon measurements are level. The most accurate way of measuring dry ingredients is to weigh them. When measuring liquids, use a clear glass or plastic jug with the metric markings.

We use large eggs with an average weight of 60g.

DRY MEASURES

METRIC	IMPERIAL
15g	½oz
30g	1oz
60g	2oz
90g	3oz
125g	4oz (¼lb)
155g	5oz
185g	6oz
220g	7oz
250g	8oz (½lb)
280g	9oz
315g	10oz
345g	11oz
375g	12oz (¾lb)
410g	13oz
440g	14oz
470g	15oz
500g	16oz (1lb)
750g	24oz (1½lb)
1kg	32oz (2lb)

LIQUID MEASURES

METRIC	IMPERIAL
30ml	1 fluid oz
60ml	2 fluid oz
100ml	3 fluid oz
125ml	4 fluid oz
150ml	5 fluid oz (¼ pint)
190ml	6 fluid oz
250ml	8 fluid oz
300ml	10 fluid oz (½ pint)
500ml	16 fluid oz
600ml	20 fluid oz (1 pint)
1000ml (1 litre)	1¾ pints

LENGTH MEASURES

METRIC	IMPERIAL
3mm	⅛in
6mm	¼in
1cm	½in
2cm	¾in
2.5cm	1in
5cm	2in
6cm	2½in
8cm	3in
10cm	4in
13cm	5in
15cm	6in
18cm	7in
20cm	8in
23cm	9in
25cm	10in
28cm	11in
30cm	12in (1ft)

OVEN TEMPERATURES

These oven temperatures are only a guide for conventional ovens. For fan-forced ovens, check the manufacturer's manual.

	°C (CELSIUS)	°F (FAHRENHEIT)	GAS MARK
Very slow	120	250	½
Slow	150	275-300	1-2
Moderately slow	160	325	3
Moderate	180	350-375	4-5
Moderately hot	200	400	6
Hot	220	425-450	7-8
Very hot	240	475	9

index

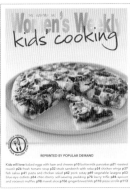

Published in 2010 by ACP Books, Sydney

ACP Books are published by ACP Magazines
a division of PBL Media Pty Limited

ACP BOOKS

General manager Christine Whiston
Editor-in-chief Susan Tomnay
Creative director & designer Hieu Chi Nguyen
Art director Hannah Blackmore
Senior editor Wendy Bryant
Food director Pamela Clark
Sales & rights director Brian Cearnes
Marketing manager Bridget Cody
Senior business analyst Rebecca Varela
Circulation manager Jama Mclean
Operations manager David Scotto
Production manager Victoria Jefferys

Published by ACP Books, a division of ACP Magazines
Ltd, 54 Park St, Sydney; GPO Box 4088, Sydney, NSW
2001.phone (02) 9282 8618; fax (02) 9267 9438.

acpbooks@acpmagazines.com.au;
www.acpbooks.com.au

Printed by Toppan Printing Co, China.

Australia Distributed by Network Services,
phone +61 2 9282 8777; fax +61 2 9264 3278;
networkweb@networkservicescompany.com.au
United Kingdom Distributed by Australian Consolidated
Press (UK), phone (01604) 642 200;
fax (01604) 642 300; books@acpuk.com
New Zealand Distributed by Netlink Distribution Company,
phone (9) 366 9966; ask@ndc.co.nz
South Africa Distributed by PSD Promotions,
phone (27 11) 392 6065/6/7; fax (27 11) 392 6079/80;
orders@psdprom.co.za
Canada Distributed by Publishers Group Canada
phone (800) 663 5714; fax (800) 565 3770;
service@raincoast.com

Title: 100 meals in minutes / food director Pamela Clark.
ISBN: 978 1 86396 992 5 (pbk.)
Notes: Includes index.
Subjects: Quick and easy cookery.
Other Authors/Contributors: Clark, Pamela.
Also Titled: Australian women's weekly.
Dewey Number: 641.555

© ACP Magazines Ltd 2010
ABN 18 053 273 546

Nutritional information Nicole Jennings
Photographer Brett Stevens
Stylist Jane Hann
Food preparation Elizabeth Macri
Cover Lamb, spinach & spiced peach salad, page 96

To order books
phone 136 116 (within Australia) or
order online at www.acpbooks.com.au
Send recipe enquiries to:
recipeenquiries@acpmagazines.com.au